The stories are light and easy to read yet hidden behind each one is the fingerprint of God's remarkable love for His children.
Clarence Johnson
Author, pastor, Bible teacher

I cruised through the book with vigor! This is real life, real Christianity -- "rubber meets the road" stuff. The authors' inclusion of verses, poems, songs and hymns make a sweet and savory read.
Lisa Murdock Padula
Teacher, speaker, radio show host, and author of *Living the Obvious Life*

These are stories of real people who have been willing to share their learning journeys with us. Their stories draw our hearts to our gracious Father in whom we find the hope and encouragement we so desperately need in these times.
Sherrie Holloway
Professor, Clarks Summit University, women's speaker, and author of *For the Love of God*

This anthology of accounts by real people offers a well of encouragement citing God's goodness and presence. I heartily commend this book to everyone -- not only to read for yourself, but to share with your family and friends.
Dr. Gary G. Cohen
Author, Biblical scholar, translator NKJV

This book was what this 73-year-old needed at this crucial time in his life. It will also be an encouragement and a blessing to you. The authors have walked with the Lord for many years, and they have something worthwhile to tell us. Take it and read it. You will not regret your effort.
Dr. William Varner
Professor, The Master's University, Sojourners Pastor, Grace Community Church, Sun Valley, CA

Foreword by Gracia Burnham,
New York Times Best Selling Author

HOPE
WHEN THE
WORLD
SHUT
DOWN

BONNIE R. PEARSON
and VICKI GOLLIHUE

WESTBOW
PRESS®
A DIVISION OF THOMAS NELSON
& ZONDERVAN

WestBow Press books may be ordered through booksellers or by contacting:

WestBow Press
A Division of Thomas Nelson & Zondervan
1663 Liberty Drive
Bloomington, IN 47403
www.westbowpress.com
844-714-3454

ISBN: 978-1-6642-0839-1 (sc)
ISBN: 978-1-6642-0840-7 (hc)
ISBN: 978-1-6642-0838-4 (e)

Library of Congress Control Number: 2020920038

Print information available on the last page.

WestBow Press rev. date: 11/10/2020

A sincere thank you to . . .

Kelly Gollihue, Erin Roten, and Anna Pearson
for their dedicated assistance to this project.

CONTENTS

FOREWORD

You hold in your hand a book of true tales and life lessons learned during a pandemic. The stories are not written by famous people or expert authors. They are written by fellow strugglers, our brothers and sisters, who never expected to add "pandemic survivor" to their resumes.

I was approached to write this foreword by authors Bonnie R. Pearson and Vicki Gollihue. Bonnie and Vicki were instrumental in the production of the play *Martin and Gracia* by Larry Belew in 2012. The play recounted the story of our year-long hostage nightmare at the hands of terrorists in the Philippine jungle, and the dramatic rescue during which my husband, Martin, was tragically killed. Bonnie directed the play, and Vicki, who was running the sound, was responsible for making sure the rescue helicopter came in at just the right time. Now Bonnie and Vicki are, once again, using their creative genius to bring us this book.

Hope When the World Shut Down is much more than just a collection of "this is what happened to me" stories. They are stories that will encourage us to persevere rather than retreat. They will inspire us to choose faith over fear. They will remind us that we are always in God's everlasting arms!

I am confident that this book will mark a trail for us to follow and encourage us as our world, again, begins to move forward on its beautiful journey.

Gracia Burnham, Author
New York Times Bestseller
In the Presence of My Enemies

DEDICATION

In memory of my mother, Sara Jean Daugherty,
for her loving example of how to be a Christ-follower, wife, and mother.
She brought joy to countless family and friends,
including Bonnie, the *Lucy* to my *Ethel*.

Mom
I miss your voice, your hugs, your smile,
and especially your stories!
Everyone loved a good *Mom* story,
so these are dedicated to you.

Vicki Gollihue
(and Bonnie R. Pearson)

INTRODUCTION

These are unusual times. A few short months ago, we went to work, visited family, ate dinner at our favorite restaurants, and went to church. We took these things for granted. The pages that follow are filled with stories of lives changed by an unexpected adversary.

Although this is an extraordinary season, it is not unprecedented. Looking to our past, people responded in a similar way during the Spanish Flu pandemic of 1918. Unable to access the technology of today, sermons were printed in local papers to encourage and teach congregants from a safe distance. To quote Rev. Fletcher Parrish of Birmingham, Alabama:

> Meditation is very profitable for the soul, but the rush of the world is so great at present that very little time is given to cogitation and reflection. Men think they have no time to walk out in the fields for contemplation, or to sit quietly by the fireside and muse.
>
> However, we have a God-given opportunity for this helpful indulgence by reason of this unique Sabbath which has dawned upon us. Out of necessity our churches are closed, and all public gatherings must be discontinued. We cannot go motoring, and we would not go to business . . . But we can sit by the fire and give ourselves to thought and reflection which will bring great profit to us. *
>
> (Used by permission. Greg Garrison. The Birmingham News. AL.com)

People are people. A hundred years later, our need to connect remains the same. Today, we have been given the gift of time to connect with God and His Word.

You will see in these stories that some quarantine experiences are shared by many. Others are unique and deeply personal. We often hesitate to reveal our private heartaches and fears. Even as Christians, we stay in our social circles, have polite conversations, and never know what others, including friends and family, may be going through.

This pandemic has changed our lives. Many have suffered loss: the loss of loved ones, the loss of jobs, and the loss of the warmth and comfort of family and friends. We miss our children, grandchildren, coworkers, and church families. I found these stories meaningful because of the insights I was able to gain from people I have never met. Their ability to find the good in difficult situations has shown me that we share more in common than we have differences.

I want to thank our contributors for opening up about their struggles and joys in these unusual, unsettling times. My prayer is that you will find meaning in these stories and be inspired as I have been.

- Vicki Gollihue

STORY 1
JOURNEY OF HOPE

I was shoulder to shoulder with people I didn't even know while grasping the pole on the monorail. Everyone was hot and sweaty from a long day. Babies were exhausted and crying. But no one was rude or unkind. That's because we all had just spent the day at the happiest place on earth—Walt Disney World. That was March 5, 2020, just eleven days before the park officially closed down.

It was one of the best weeks of my life. My immediate family rented a house in Florida. Together we enjoyed a day in Disney, a grand sixtieth anniversary party for my parents, and eightieth birthday celebration for my Dad.

While there we became concerned when we noticed the store was out of tissues and hand sanitizer. The check-out lines at Walmart were long—even at 10:00 p.m. No one was at the point of alarm just yet, or so I thought.

We had a wonderful week together celebrating, hugging, and taking lots of pictures. I'm grateful that the Lord gave all of us the opportunity to be with family before the world shut down.

Nearly overnight, I went from eating all my meals with my grandchildren to reading stories to them remotely on video chats. I went from performing live concerts to recording music videos and posting them on Facebook. Life wasn't horrible, but sometimes I felt suffocated.

Although I was barred from going out to places and seeing the people I loved, no one could put bars on my imagination. I found my freedom through working on creative projects—writing songs and stories. And so, this collection of snapshots of people's lives was born. It gave me hope to write. It gave me hope as I read the stories that others wrote of their quarantine journeys.

May these stories also refresh *your* soul, bringing you encouragement, joy, and hope, wherever your journey has taken you.

"We have this hope as an anchor for the soul, firm and secure."—Hebrews 6:19-20 NIV

Bonnie R. Pearson, Erial, NJ, USA
Author, *Hope When the World Shut Down*

"Where there's hope there's life. It fills us with fresh courage and makes us strong again."
—Anne Frank

STORY 2
GOD WILL MAKE A WAY

"I don't think you want to go in there!" the young man said, running up to our car.

I was looking forward to a fun-filled reception. We had just left the church where my beautiful daughter, Casey, had gotten married. Family pictures were taken, and my sisters had escorted my mother to the reception hall. So why were we being met by this man with a tragic look on his face? Looking past him, I saw an ambulance, and my heart sank. I ran inside to see the unthinkable. My mom was on the floor with EMTs trying to resuscitate her frail body.

Everyone was crying. All we could think to do was gather around her and sing Mom's favorite song, "In the Garden." That's when I had to go back across the street to give the news to my daughter. She was heartbroken. This was her wedding day!

In the months before, I had been home in New Jersey with my mom making plans for Casey's Ohio wedding. Although Mom was ninety years old, she was in good health and was determined to make the trip. I never guessed I would spend the drive home planning her funeral. It was all very sad and surreal.

Then three weeks later, my son got married, and we became empty nesters. Three months after that, we lost my dear mother-in-law, and quickly after, we even lost our sweet dog, Daisy.

There was already much loss in my life when the pandemic hit. My husband and I both lost our jobs. With finances tight, and still grieving, there were days I didn't think I would make it. But even on the hardest days, I knew deep down that God was still with me. He saw us through each day, supplied our needs, and comforted me through one of the most difficult times of my life. I often think of Don Moen's lyrics, "God will make a way where there seems to be no way. He works in ways we cannot see; He will make a way for me."

And He continues to make a way.

"Casting all your anxieties on him, because he cares for you."—1 Peter 5:7 ESV

Vicki Gollihue, Erial, NJ, USA
Author, *Hope When the World Shut Down*

God Will Make A Way

Oh, God will make a way
Where there seems to be no way,
He works in ways we cannot see
He will make a way for me.
He will be my guide
Hold me closely to His side,
With love and strength for each new day
He will make a way, He will make a way.

"Behold, I am doing a new thing;
now it springs forth, do you not perceive it?
I will make a way in the wilderness
and rivers in the desert."

Isaiah 43:19 ESV

STORY 3
PRECIOUS MOMENTS

As an English teacher in Japan, my school year runs from April to March. Just days before my students were set to graduate, the coronavirus hit our island, starting the first big outbreak in Japan. Restrictions began quickly. Graduation, while allowed to continue, was limited to only the graduates and teachers. Our huge gymnasium had already been decorated. Chairs for family members, important guests, and other students filled the room. On graduation day, my students filed through the sea of empty chairs, the twenty-five staff members' applause was the only sound in the hollow room.

Graduations in Japan are somber ceremonies, but no one could have anticipated the heaviness that filled the room. My heart broke looking at my disappointed students, blindsided right before this day that they had long anticipated. It's hard enough saying goodbye to my students, but this was certainly not how I wanted the school year to end. It was especially hard after the ceremony when I went to say my goodbyes. I was able to spend final precious moments with these students I loved. I cried with them, laughed with them, and sat with them in disappointment.

During this time, I've seen how powerful it is to share in the pain and disappointment of others. I was dealing with disappointment myself. I had to cancel a long-anticipated trip, my family could no longer visit Japan, and my new school year plans were shattered. But as I received comfort from the Lord and let go of my disappointment, I found myself better able to share that comfort with others who were hurting. Even from vast distances, I could see the Lord's peace and comfort spread as I talked with friends who were all dealing with their own pain.

I don't have the power to take away hurt, but my God is the great healer and comforter. As His people, we can be vessels of His peace and comfort. As you accept His comfort, allow it to radiate from you and bring peace and healing to those around you.

"Praise be to the God and Father of our Lord Jesus Christ, the Father of compassion and the God of all comfort, who comforts us in all our troubles, so that we can comfort those in any trouble with the comfort we ourselves receive from God. For just as we share abundantly in the sufferings of Christ, so also our comfort abounds through Christ."—2 Corinthians 1:3-5 NIV

Hannah Hayden, Higashikawa, Hokkaido, Japan
Wife, ESL teacher

STORY 4
FINDING PERSPECTIVE

The coronavirus has brought the world to a virtual standstill and affected the lifestyle of every individual and family. It can sometimes be hard to discern between real threats and hysteria. People are reacting in very different ways. Some use the quarantine to spend more time with family, pray and read the Scriptures, and enjoy the quietness of life. For some, it has caused a rise in depression and abuse.

Let's put this period of time into perspective. The pandemic has only been with us for about three months. For some, it seems like a lifetime. Imagine for a moment that you were born in the year 1900.

- On your fourteenth birthday, World War I begins, then ends when you turn eighteen. Twenty-two million people perish in that war.
- Later that year, a Spanish Flu pandemic hits and runs until your twentieth birthday. Fifty million people die during those two years with five-hundred million people infected. Yes, fifty million perished!
- On your twenty-ninth birthday, the Great Depression begins and lasts until you are thirty-three. Unemployment hits 25 percent and the World GDP drops 27 percent. The country nearly collapses along with the world economy.
- When you turn thirty-nine, World War II starts. By your forty-first birthday, the United States is pulled into WWII. Between your thirty-ninth and forty-fifth birthday, seventy-five million people perish in the war.
- At fifty, the Korean War starts. Five million perish.
- At fifty-five, the Vietnam War begins and doesn't end for twenty years! Four million people perish in that conflict.

- On your sixty-second birthday the Cuban Missile Crisis happens, a tipping point in the Cold War. Life on our planet, as we know it, should have ended. Great leaders prevented that from happening.
- When you turn seventy-five, the Vietnam War finally ends.

Now you can understand when your grandparents speak about "when times were hard." And they survived!

What we are experiencing right now has lasted for a *few months*! We need to keep things in perspective and remember that God knows exactly what is going on. He will watch over us and keep us safe!

"The Lord will keep you from all harm – He will watch over your life; the Lord will watch over your coming and going both now and forevermore."—Psalm 121:7-8 NIV

Richard Muller, Ridgewood, NJ, USA
Health and wellness teacher and three-season coach for thirty-four years

STORY 5
EXTRA BUFFALO SAUCE

At last, the moment I had been anticipating had arrived. I was excited. I was eager. I was hungry. It was time to unwrap and eat the sandwich that I had just brought home. This sandwich, with each ingredient carefully selected for the ultimate sandwich experience, always causes me to do a little happy dance when I sit down to eat it. Yes, really.

I carefully pulled the tape on the wrapper, moving the order slip showing each ingredient I had ordered. To my surprise and great disappointment, the sandwich revealed was far from the one I had ordered. It was dripping with buffalo sauce, which is not on my list of carefully selected ingredients. My next thought was one of sadness, knowing that the person who ordered this sandwich might experience the same disappointment receiving my perfect sandwich. Maybe the garlic aioli that I like triggers the same response in them that the buffalo sauce did in me.

I considered the situation the world is in right now—one of disappointment and inconvenience to say the least, but also one of fear, death, destruction, and great loss. My sandwich struggles began to lose their significance. Paul, a great disciple of Jesus, experienced almost every kind of pain imaginable, and still said "I have learned in whatever situation I am to be content" (Phil. 4:11 ESV). Surely if Paul faced shipwreck, persecution, and beatings and still remained content, then I have no reason not to be content in every circumstance, even when I unwrap a sandwich that isn't the one I ordered. My thoughts turned to gratitude to be able to purchase a warm, healthy sandwich, and eat it in my safe home with my loving husband. Suddenly, that extra buffalo sauce wasn't so bad.

"Not that I am speaking of being in need, for I have learned in whatever situation I am to be content. I know how to be brought low, and I know how to abound. In any and every circumstance, I have learned the secret of facing plenty and hunger, abundance and need."—Philippians 4:11-12 ESV

Jen Whylings, Bethlehem, PA, USA
Wife, paralegal, and sandwich enthusiast

GOD WILL PROVIDE

"I need you to turn in your keys."

I sat there stunned for a moment. I knew we were headed in that direction, but my general manager's words hit me like a ton of bricks. It was mid-March and as the pandemic was growing, I had been holding out hope that somehow our store wouldn't have to close. It was just a few short days before my interview for front of house manager at the restaurant where I was working as a server. As I turned in my keys, I was angry that I had just lost my source of income. I had worked hard and had become a trusted and reliable employee.

Along with the stress of unemployment and paying bills, I was chasing after an active toddler and trying to help my seven-year-old son with his online learning and coping skills. The schools had closed, and he missed his friends and teacher! My husband was able to keep his job which helped a lot, but the pressure was overwhelming. Sometimes I just hid in the shower and cried.

However, God tells me in Psalm 56 that He has collected all my tears in His bottle. He indeed heard my cries as I was given temporary employment at a local supermarket. What I didn't know was that when my restaurant was finally able to reopen, the coveted front of house manager position I had applied for had been eliminated. Because I was still a server, I was able to return to work, even getting an unprecedented $140.00 in tips on the first night. God in His wisdom had protected me, as He knew what was ahead. Thank goodness He is the one in control and not me!

"Look at the birds of the air: they neither sow nor reap nor gather into barns, and yet your heavenly Father feeds them. Are you not of more value than they? And which of you by being anxious can add a single hour to his span of life?"—Matthew 6:26-27 ESV

Elizabeth P., Leesburg, FL, USA
Wife, mother, and restaurant server

STORY 7
HIDDEN GIFTS

I once wrote a chapel talk called "Gifts I Never Asked For." It was inspired by the childhood disappointment of one particular Christmas morning. I had asked for only one thing—the LP movie soundtrack of *The Sound of Music*. I saw the right-sized package under the tree and fully anticipated having my hopes rewarded—only to open the gift and find the Broadway musical soundtrack.

I was crushed, but I could not let on. I knew my parents thought they had given me exactly what I had asked for. Eventually, I actually came to value songs on the Broadway version that were not in the movie version.

This experience became something of a motif for my journey. I don't mean that I am a Pollyanna or artificially cheery about life's disappointing expectations. I also don't subscribe to theological explanations that tie the world's pain, or my own pain, directly to God's planning. Rather, I have learned that, in any circumstances that come to us, there are hidden surprises—good things that would not otherwise have come our way.

I am slowly coming to see the gifts hidden deep within this COVID-19 season. I say this cautiously. For one thing, we are still in the middle of this. Secondly, the range of pain is great, and I don't want to speak in a way that seems to trivialize anyone's pain.

In spite of this, even now, I want to be bold enough to name some of the gifts that I see. I hear co-workers talk about the extra time they are having with their children. And as a college, this pandemic is pushing us to a level of intensified imagination and innovation that we would not have embraced voluntarily—and of which we would not have thought ourselves capable.

In the midst of your own journey today, may you glimpse some hint of a *gift* that you would never have asked for—and yet, having received, would not ever think of exchanging.

"We know that all things work together for good for those who love God, who are called according to his purpose."—Romans 8:28 NRSV

Shirley A. Mullen, Houghton, NY, USA
President, Houghton College

STORY 8
WAKE UP!

"Get ready to rethink everything you thought ministry was. I have something new for you." God was speaking to me loud and clear. I was newly married and had just taken a position as NextGen pastor at a church in Queens, New York City. I already had years of experience in ministry and was sure I knew what that looked like.

It was a great time of change for us. In just a few months' time, my wife and I had gotten married, moved to New York, started new positions, and adopted two amazing senior dogs. Little did we know that we would quickly begin a season of even more challenges.

We had been serving at our new church for three months when we found ourselves in lockdown and living in the epicenter of the pandemic. Sunday services went online and youth meetings were held over video chats. I had been looking forward to planning this year's vacation Bible school and Easterfest, a well-attended community event. But now, everything was cancelled! My amazing year of ministry quickly turned into something completely different. How could I minister to young people when I couldn't even be with them in the same room? This was when it got interesting, and everything changed—again.

God was going to teach me a lesson about new and creative ways to reach out to kids. Suddenly, my job was not event oriented, it was production oriented. My skill set expanded as I learned about the tech of recording and producing Sunday morning videos. I had to use my imagination to teach and preach the gospel to kids through the lens of a camera.

This time of ministry has taught me things I never thought I would learn six months ago, or a lifetime ago. Jesus calls us to be in community, not plan events. Jesus calls us to grow deeper in relationships with believers, to equip His people, to reach out to those who don't believe, and to grow deeper into relationship with Him. God has changed my understanding of what a pastoral position looks like. He has called me to wake up!

"Awake, O sleeper, and arise from the dead, and Christ will shine on you."—Ephesians 5:14 ESV

Kevin Gollihue, Freeport, NY, USA
Pastor in Queens, New York City

'Necessary Action'

"By the wise and necessary action of the City Commission and the Board of Health, on account of the scourge of disease now prevailing, all congregational activities are canceled for a minimum period of two weeks. But, while this providence is a severe one, affecting as it does all our plans and programs in this the most opportune season of the entire church year, may we not yet turn this season to best account by accepting it as an opportunity for the exercise of a fuller devotion to God and to the things of His Kingdom? Necessarily we shall be kept in our homes many hours that would otherwise be spent in recreation and amusement.

Perhaps this circumstance will serve to remind us that in these sacred home-circles there is to be found the very finest of fellowship and the sweetest and most wholesome of all influences. And certainly if we should improve these hours by prayer and meditation, the seeming curse of this scourge would not be unmixed with blessing."

Rev. S.O. Coxe, Pastor
Handley Memorial Presbyterian Church
Birmingham, Alabama
1918
(Used by permission. Greg Garrison.
The Birmingham News. AL.com)

STORY 9
PEEK-A-BOO!

"Wanna play peek-a-boo?" And the game is on! My beautiful grandson's face is beaming at me from more than 200 miles away. Facetime has been my friend since the shutdown, and I'm grateful. Without this technology, I would never get to play with Josiah or see his perfectly adorable face. We've dubbed these visits "Hot Chocolate with Grandma." But I miss the in-person visits with this little guy and his brand new baby brother. I miss hugs, snuggles with the baby, and Josiah's bubbly personality as he bounces around the room.

The global pandemic has stopped our lives for too long. Many of us grow tired of the isolation, not seeing our loved ones, friends and church family. I am a rebel and make sure that I visit my local farm market regularly, as I did before the stay-at-home order. My Amish friends are there, and I am comfortable there, but the market is only open at half capacity and we are social distancing. "Well worth the wait," I say to myself as I stand in line outside the front doors.

I started regular posts on Facebook of everyday joys. A simple image or thought could uplift my circle of friends and remind them that there is still good in the world. I regularly FaceTime my sisters and attend Zoom meetings for Bible study. I've learned that community is important and to be grateful for the technology that keeps us connected. This was a lesson I had already learned, but this time of quarantine was God's reminder that we need each other. We wait to be together again, and when we are, we will love and appreciate each other just a little bit more. A hard lesson to learn, but there is good in the waiting.

"And let us consider how we may spur one another on toward love and good deeds, not giving up meeting together, as some are in the habit of doing, but encouraging one another—and all the more as you see the Day approaching."—Hebrews 10:24-25 NIV

Joy Geer, Berlin, NJ, USA
Proud mom of four handsome men, grandma of two beautiful boys!

STORY 10
FEAR IN THE AIRWAVES

At first, news stories reported that only China had been hit by the virus. Later, we saw that it had started spreading to other parts of the world. The number of deaths recorded in Italy really got my attention. I began to be concerned as the government in Ghana, where I live, announced that our borders were going to be closed immediately. Soon the mainstream media began to trumpet fear in the airwaves.

The idea that the virus had no vaccine also gave me much concern. I started asking myself, "Will I live to finish God's plan for my life?" I listened to the news about how quickly the virus was spreading, and how the death count was rapidly rising. The more I listened, the more I worried. I came to realize that my worry was based on my faith in the data and the predictions of possible deaths that could happen. As I began to shift my focus from the news to God's Word, I was reminded of the truth of the essence of God.

If God knows everything from the beginning to the end, and if He knew that I was going to live in such a time, then why am I worrying? The more I began to concentrate on God's Word, my worries subsided.

If faith comes by hearing, and hearing by the word of God, then fear is inevitable when we are no longer listening to the Word of God. Scripture tells us that God has not given us the spirit of fear. The pandemic has taught me how important it is to continually trust in God's Word as the only way to handle adversity.

"When I am afraid, I put my trust in you. In God, whose word I praise, in God I trust; I shall not be afraid . . ."—Psalm 56:3-4 ESV

Cyprian Antwi Awuah, Accra, Ghana
Bold Grace Ministries

STORY 11
UNEXPECTED BLESSINGS!

It was midnight on March 9, 2020, and way too early for me to be up. I slid behind the wheel of my car, my coffee-spiked hot chocolate in hand. My oldest daughter, who had spent spring break in Montreal, was now returning home. After picking her up from the Syracuse airport, Caetlynn said she thought it was odd that the border patrol asked if she had a temperature or cough. She wondered why he said, "Americans going to Canada are the real problem."

Two days later my son, Michael, messaged me from his college in Ohio. "What?" I took a second look at my phone. "Picked up tomorrow?" I arrived early at the pickup location, a grocery store, and stopped in to shop. The empty shelves were noticeable. As I emerged from the store, Michael's ride pulled up. "That was a quick semester!" I quipped as he got into my car.

Next, daughter number two messaged me. She was coming home from her college in Illinois next week. Then my husband announced that he was going to start working from home.

The more the merrier, I thought. Right? I'm a teacher and was already preparing to teach online from home. My youngest son, Christopher, a high school student, was gearing up to work online at home as well.

I realized that it had been ages since all of us had been together for an extended period of time. We each hide away in our corners, busy with papers, conference calls, presentations, and classes, but when we get together there is always laughter and joy. I treasure every moment! Unexpected blessings!

"Children are a gift from the LORD; they are a reward from him."—Psalm 127:3 NLT

Deborah de Oliveira, Horseheads, NY, USA
Wife, mother of four, teacher

STORY 12

SONGS AT MIDNIGHT

My worst moments always come in the dead of night. I don't like the dreary silence. The darkness is oppressive. The aloneness of being quarantined is overwhelming.

One such night, I instinctively reached out for my guitar. I strummed a few random chords and listened as the notes echoed in my room. I was prompted to play a little more. The sound was soothing. I was amazed at the calming effect!

In a moment of clarity, I remembered some lyrics my friend had written and had left at my studio. It was about looking to God for hope in hopeless times. With guitar in hand and with my mind focused on creating music, I began composing a melody. In a very short time, I had written the complete ballad.

Suddenly, the blackness of the night didn't seem so menacing. The midnight gloom had given way to a song of praise. Sometimes God works small miracles in life through the gift of music.

"Around midnight Paul and Silas were praying and singing hymns to God, and the other prisoners were listening to them. Suddenly there was such a violent earthquake that the foundations of the prison were shaken. At once all the prison doors flew open, and everyone's chains came loose."—Acts 16:25-26 NIV

Mariano Jose Jimenez, Ventnor City, NJ, USA
Musician

Hold Me in Your Hope
Hebrews 6:19; 11:1

When I awake and reality's no dream,
And when my life isn't really what it seems,
My world is caught on pause making me afraid.
My world is caught on pause; I'm feeling suffocated.

Never thought I'd see this craziness in life.
Only in books I'd read had I seen this kind of strife.
Now when it counts, Lord, I could really use your strength.
Now when it counts, Lord, I could really see your face.

Hold me in your hope when everything is surreal,
No matter how hopeless I feel.
Hold me in your hope, I'm making one last appeal.
Help me survive this ordeal.

We have this hope, an anchor for the soul.
Firm and secure, things hoped for.

Now I'm sitting here, the days all in a blur,
Waiting on you, gazing out the door.
Watching the days crawl, your promises come true.
Watching the days crawl, I'm looking up to you.

STORY 13
WHERE ARE YOU?

God, where are you? How can you allow these terrible things to happen? Do you even care?

Have you asked these questions? The months during the pandemic were difficult and just plain strange! My husband and I were both deemed "essential workers." I work in a grocery store and he works in food manufacturing. I understand that food is essential, but having people thank me on a daily basis for coming into work was just not normal! I saw the fear and anxiety in their demeanor. I heard the worry in their voices. I prayed that God would use me to be a light in the darkness—that people would see Jesus in me and be comforted. As Christians, we are the only Jesus some will ever see!

Around this time, we also found out that our six-month-old grandson had been diagnosed with a genetic syndrome that compromised his health. We didn't understand why this had to happen to him. I will never know this side of Heaven, but I do know that God wants us to trust Him. He created the universe and knows what He's doing! He loves my grandson even more than I do.

Sitting in the car one day, waiting for my husband to come out of a store, I just had it with God. I yelled. I cried out. I begged and pleaded. He felt so far away.

"Where are you, Lord?"

I then saw my husband coming out of the store with a strange look on his face. He got in the car and said, "You will never guess what song was playing in the store! 'His Eye is on the Sparrow and I know He watches me.'" This wasn't even a Christian store! I broke down in tears of joy and a peace came over me. That was Abba, my Father, reassuring me that He heard me and was watching over me and my family. In that moment, I was reminded of the meaning behind my grandson Josiah's name—"God is healer." Coincidence? I think not. God has big plans for him!

"What is the price of two sparrows – one copper coin? But not a single sparrow can fall to the ground without our Father knowing it."— Matthew 10:29 NLT

Cindy Nelson, Springfield, MA, USA
Mom of two, grandmother of three

His Eye Is on the Sparrow

Why should I feel discouraged,
Why should the shadows come,
Why should my heart be lonely,
And long for heaven and home,
When Jesus is my portion?
My constant friend is He:
His eye is on the sparrow,
And I know He watches me;
His eye is on the sparrow,
And I know He watches me.

I sing because I'm happy,
I sing because I'm free,
For His eye is on the sparrow,
And I know He watches me.

"Let not your heart be troubled,"
His tender word I hear,
And resting on His goodness,
I lose my doubts and fears;
Though by the path He leadeth,
But one step I may see;
His eye is on the sparrow,
And I know He watches me;
His eye is on the sparrow,
And I know He watches me.

I sing because I'm happy,
I sing because I'm free,
For his eye is on the sparrow,
And I know He watches me.

(Civilla D. Martin. 1905. Public Domain)

STORY 14
KINDNESS OF STRANGERS

The pandemic made us hungry. Hungry for knowledge, statistics, money, masks, sanitizer, toilet paper, hair dye, and for some, the love and comfort of our Lord and Savior. As a doctor battling this crisis every day, I saw firsthand the chaos in our hospitals. During this time, an unusual marriage was formed between restaurants and hospitals. The restaurant industry, stricken with an abundance of food and a lack of customers, granted comfort to hospital workers with daily meals. Local eateries were filled with food in a time of closures and furloughs. As a result, each unit in my hospital had lunch, and often breakfast, for about forty-five days because of this unusual pairing of necessity and the kindness of strangers.

One particular day, a family member was seen in the lobby—a rarity during times of quarantine. She noticed all the food coming in and asked my nurse if anything extra remained. Two beautifully boxed lunches were gladly given to this hungry visitor. In her excitement and gratitude, she showered blessings on us for this generous gesture, proclaiming, "The Lord bless you and your families!" Moments later, another staff member, looking outside, noticed the boxes being shared among five or six people outside on a bench.

It saddened us that despite being entrenched in a "war zone" with patient beds overflowing into hallways and cafeterias, bigger battles raged on yards away. Just outside, families went moment to moment, looking for a way to comfort their children's rumbling stomachs. As the story spread, within seven days, the hospital was able to arrange for a weekly food pantry for locals looking for that small piece of hope and satisfaction. The Lord blesses us in many ways, and we know to "look at the birds of the air; they do not sow or reap or store away in barns, and yet your heavenly Father feeds them" (Matt. 6:26 NIV). Our gracious and omniscient Father is with us and guiding all our steps daily.

"For I was hungry and you gave me food, I was thirsty and you gave me drink, I was a stranger and you welcomed me."—Matthew 25:35 ESV

Sunil George, M.D., Long Island, NY, USA
Husband, father, and dog dad

STORY 15
LESSONS FROM A RIVER

On a beautiful spring weekend, my wife, Jane, and I sat along the Delaware River to have a picnic. As we ate our lunch, I thought about how peaceful and quiet it was, knowing that desperation was being felt in many hospitals in Philadelphia, New York City, and throughout the world. These places may be far away in distance, but they are close in heart, knowing the anxieties and stresses of the coronavirus and COVID-19.

The Delaware has flowed through all of earth's crises and history. It flowed before Europeans ever arrived, and long before the indigenous peoples fished its waters. It flowed when Washington's small army crossed over on Christmas Eve in 1776, just south of where we were sitting. It flowed during the Civil War, the Spanish flu, polio epidemics, the Great Depression, two World Wars, the Korean War, the Vietnam War, the Gulf War, the AIDS epidemic, the endless war on terror and now, COVID-19.

The river flows as it has since Creation, or at least since the Flood. It will continue to flow when you and I have long since left this world. As it moves toward the sea, it informs us that it is more permanent than our own stay on earth.

We grip this life with such desperation as though it were our own when it is not. This life is simply, as the British would say, a *lay-by* on the way to eternity, and a brief one at that. This makes every moment of our lives meaningful, significant, and not to be wasted. Our time here is preparation for our real existence that lasts forever after this one is over. What you and I do with our lives in serving Christ is significant.

This time of shutdown has its challenges, but with a wider field of view, we can see that it is a time of opportunity. Let's redeem that time and seize the opportunity to be what God has transformed us to be, and to do what He left us here to do—make disciples of all nations!

"Teach us to number each of our days so that we may grow in wisdom."—Psalm 90:12 GW

Douglas K. Batchelder, Phillipsburg, NJ, USA
Missions Board Advancement Officer

STORY 16
FAMILY GAME NIGHT

Charades. Scattergories. Quiplash. Guesstures. Mario Kart. Puzzles.

"Family Game Night." Three of my favorite words!

In 1 Thessalonians 5:18 NKJV, Paul wrote, "In everything give thanks." Not give thanks *for* everything, but give thanks *in* everything. God has been teaching me how to be thankful in the midst of a challenging season.

This current situation has allowed me to spend additional time with my family. One day I'll look back fondly, not on COVID-19, but on all the time this pandemic has allowed (forced) us to have together. Even now, I've enjoyed the relaxed pace around the house, family game nights, shared meals, and unhurried discussions.

I'm also thankful for greater opportunities to share the gospel. Friends I haven't heard from in years have watched sermons and asked questions, allowing me to share Christ with them. This would have been unimaginable just a few months ago.

This pandemic has made me realize how much I take for granted. Jeremiah wrote that God's mercies "are new every morning" (Lam. 3:23 ESV). Many days I don't even notice God's mercies. I'm certainly more aware of them now and hopefully I'll continue to notice and thank God for them in the future.

We live in a broken world. Romans 8 tells us that all of creation groans. The same chapter tells us that God works all things together for good. This world is like a mosaic. Even though it's broken, as we allow God to put the pieces together, we can see beauty in the brokenness.

"For we know that the whole creation groans and labors with birth pangs together until now."—Romans 8:22 NKJV

"And we know that all things work together for good to those who love God, to those who are the called according to His purpose."—Romans 8:28 NKJV

Rick L., Laurel Springs, NJ, USA
Husband, father, and pastor

"All this is for your benefit, so that the grace that is reaching more and more people may cause thanksgiving to overflow to the glory of God." —2 Corinthians 4:15 NIV

STORY 17
TULIPS

The line had gotten so long, we had to turn off the motor of the car. No, we weren't in line at a restaurant drive thru. We weren't even waiting to see a Phillies game or fireworks on the Fourth of July. We were in line to see a field of tulips!

It was a partly sunny Sunday in mid-April, and everyone was itching to do something fun during the heart of the pandemic. No one waiting in the line of cars seemed impatient. No one was honking or looking aggravated. No one had anywhere else to go—no place to rush off to. Children popped their heads out of sunroofs. Others banged pots and pans in celebration or played with shiny pinwheels. Dogs of all sizes were hanging out of rolled-down windows. There was a feeling of unity as everyone anticipated seeing something beautiful to brighten their day.

When it was finally our turn, we started up the car and began driving through the farm. We wanted to drink in everything there was to see—absorb every minute of our outing—and enjoy the flowers bursting with color all around us. We drove slowly, stopping often to lean out the window and take pictures.

Each blossom was beautiful. Some were in rows by color. Other clusters dotted the field in bright color combinations. Although we waited an hour in the car, the actual tour only lasted about ten minutes. But it was worth it. It made me smile just to relax without the pressure of a schedule to keep. As we drove out of the farm, I was excited to purchase a bouquet of pink tulips as a reminder of our perfect day.

It was wonderful to just "stop and smell the tulips."

"Behold, what I have seen to be good and fitting is to eat and drink and find enjoyment in all the toil with which one toils under the sun the few days of his life that God has given him, for this is his lot."—Ecclesiastes 5:18 ESV

Bonnie R. Pearson, Erial, NJ, USA
Author, *Hope When the World Shut Down*

". . . *See how the flowers of the field grow. They do not labor or spin. Yet I tell you that not even Solomon in all his splendor was dressed like one of these."—Matthew 6:28-29 NIV*

Like a Sunday in the Park

Sleeping in through the pouring rain,
Pancake breakfasts with bacon and eggs,
Nights by the fire just playing board games . . .

Walking the dog, waving as you go,
In the fresh air with the kids in tow.
Dinner together, new recipes,
Take your time, nowhere to be.
Having Sunday dinner on a Thursday night,
Go to the field just to fly a kite.

Like a Sunday in the park again.

- Bonnie R. Pearson

STORY 18
DISTRACTIONS

It's not as easy to run away from your problems when your distractions are limited. When America began to shut down at the end of March 2020, I could no longer hide my struggle with anxiety. Though my faith was strong in the summer of 2019, I began spending less time with God in the fall. I began to focus more on problems with school, work, and my relationships. About a week after stores and schools closed, I realized it was getting more difficult to distract myself.

My anxiety caught up to me and suddenly I felt trapped and overwhelmed. Though it wasn't easy, I went to my parents and told them that I had been struggling with anxiety and depression. Not long afterward, I was surrounded by people who love me—my parents, sister, boyfriend, and neighbor, who were giving me words of encouragement and love. I felt so blessed to be in the presence of love during such uncertain times. The comfort they gave came from the peace that only God can provide. This reminded me that I could take hold of my anxiety by returning to the One who helped me face it in the first place. If I want to receive the peace of God, I need to come to Him with my worries instead of trying to distract myself from them.

Since that night, I have been spending more time praying, studying the Bible, and reading devotionals. His peace has helped me to combat the anxieties of my life and the events going on in the world. In order to continue receiving His peace, I know that I must keep coming to Him even when the quarantine is over and the distractions of life set in.

"Do not be anxious about anything, but in every situation, by prayer and petition, with thanksgiving, present your requests to God. And the peace of God, which transcends all understanding, will guard your hearts and your minds in Christ Jesus."—Philippians 4:6-7 NIV

Alyssa Barrett, Stratford, NJ, USA
College Student

STORY 19
THE STILL PRESENCE OF GOD

Will business ever return to normal? It was mid-March and our company's events began to be cancelled. By April, my wife and I began to realize that something major was happening. We had owned and operated this business for seven years. Now we were wondering how much our business would be changed, maybe permanently.

With a rambunctious three-year-old and a sleepless eight-month-old, "time off" did not exist. How I spent my time was quickly and dramatically shifting. One week I'm booking events, training employees, ordering inventory, making bank deposits, paying invoices, putting out drama fires, and the next week, there's nothing! Now we have days filled with diaper changes, playtime, meal planning, budgeting, disciplining, and well, basically full-time parenting.

I learned quickly to appreciate my wife's skills more than ever. Actually, this is possibly the best thing that could have happened to our family. Before the pandemic there was something unhealthy about the way I balanced my business and family. We both knew it. I always felt we could never keep up with the growing demands of each one. The "divine disruption," as I like to call it, didn't make everything perfect, but it has certainly given us time to start figuring out a better way. And we've been able to create priceless family memories.

In the busyness of our culture, I can hear God say, "Be still, and know that I am God" (Ps. 46:10 KJV). Let's position ourselves to receive God's blessing of sovereign grace. Here are three practical ways that have helped me on that journey.

First, cling to moments of joy. Be present. You may need to put the phone away for an hour. If you're spending valuable time with your family, truly be with them and capture the joy in the moments.

Next, search for opportunity in the storm. Every challenge we face is an opportunity to grow and change what we thought was normal, and ultimately get closer to Christ.

And last, create new habits that help center your life around God. Right now, we have an opportunity to prepare ourselves for the next chapter of our lives. We have been given the precious gift of time!

"Come, see the glorious works of the Lord: See how he brings destruction upon the world. He causes wars to end throughout the earth. He breaks the bow and snaps the spear; he burns the shields with fire. Be still, and know that I am God!"—Psalm 46:8-10 NLT

Tim Pearson, Philadelphia, PA, USA
Owner of Top Hat Espresso Catering, husband, and father of two

STORY 20
DEEPER INTIMACY

Before the COVID-19 pandemic, I was able to leave the house at any time. Now, even as a police officer, I could only leave for my eight-hour shift unless it was absolutely essential. The coffee shops where I enjoyed researching and working on my computer were closed. My gym was shut down indefinitely and my second job was no longer available. I was concerned about the loss of my additional income and the lack of access to the entertainment to which I had grown accustomed.

As time passed in quarantine, I began to see the truth about those things I had lost. They were distractions! I had become dependent on having extra money. I needed the places to go and things to do as fillers for my soul. They distracted me from the emptiness that comes with being still.

The Bible is clear that this world only offers emptiness and discontentment. No worldly possession can fill the God-shaped vacuum that is in every human being. I began to experience that reality once the distractions were removed from my life. This was an opportunity to reach a deeper intimacy with the Lord Jesus.

I began by imagining what it might be like if I was confined to a wheelchair or bedridden. Would I be alone, bored, or empty? Then I remembered that God has indwelled me with His Holy Spirit. I am born again and His child forever. So, I formed the next logical deduction— Jesus is always with me! I immediately felt the anxiety leave and I experienced the peace that only God can provide. I realized that God gives us things to enjoy such as money, hobbies, and relationships. But only the truth of Jesus' eternal presence brings the peace I desire.

"Keep your life free from love of money, and be content with what you have, for he has said, "I will never leave you nor forsake you.""—Hebrews 13:5 ESV

Charlie Eipper, Wichita Falls, TX, USA
Patrol Sergeant, Wichita Falls Police Department

STORY 21
UNCLEAN!

"Unclean! Unclean!"

Luke 17 tells the story of Jesus being met by ten lepers who asked for healing. Lepers had to live in isolation and call out "unclean" whenever someone came near. These men had a contagious disease that everyone feared, and there was no cure. Medical experts now believe leprosy is transmitted via droplets from the nose or mouth during close and frequent contact with the ill person.

Fast forward to January 2020 when the world we knew was about to change. We began to hear about a new coronavirus spreading throughout the world. COVID-19 is contracted through human contact via coughing, sneezing, or touch, and there is no cure. As a registered nurse working in a hospital, I began to see COVID-19 cases entering our facility. The first emergency on our unit shook me to the core! The virus was here, and we were in the battle.

My son and daughter-in-law arranged for me to spend one last morning with my twin grandchildren before I would have direct contact with COVID-19 patients. At the end of our visit, as I listened to a favorite song on the radio, I froze and began to weep. Was I going to die and never see my precious grandchildren again? When my pity party was over, I pulled myself together realizing that God is all powerful and He would never leave me or forsake me.

I recall entering a bank in March and requesting to wear my mask. I explained that my mask was to protect them because I worked with COVID-19 patients. The tellers were upset and too fearful to deal with me. Only one teller encouraged me to come to him, and he professionally completed my transaction. Only one person chose to help me. Only one person wasn't afraid. The others viewed me as "unclean!"

Yes, I take care of patients who are placed in an isolation room with no family or visitors allowed. I can only imagine how it must feel to be alone, sick, and afraid of a disease with no cure. But when Jesus reached out His hand and touched the lepers, He demonstrated love, compassion, and acceptance. Shouldn't we do the same?

"Finally, all of you, be like-minded, be sympathetic, love one another, be compassionate and humble."—1 Peter 3:8 NIV

Lynn Stott, Stratford, NJ, USA
Nurse, mother, and grandmother of twin girls

STORY 22
NO POMP AND CIRCUMSTANCE

You dream for twenty years of graduating college. Everything leads up to the moment you walk across that stage. Celebrating with friends and saying last goodbyes is what keeps you going, but the Class of 2020 was deprived of this important milestone. Yes, we got our diplomas, but what we were looking forward to was the ending. This unexpected ending was too abrupt. On that Friday morning in March, we were all expecting news about how the coronavirus would affect our school. I woke up to an email that said we were required to leave campus in just six days. No one knew how to handle the situation, or their emotions—especially the seniors. We would suddenly have to say goodbye to the place we had called home for four years. It felt like sudden death! By Tuesday, most people were already off campus. I knew it was time to leave. Doing schoolwork at home without friends around and no set schedule was difficult. I wasn't motivated to do anything. Slowly but surely, I got my work done, kept in contact with friends, and before I knew it, it was time for virtual graduation.

So where is the light in all this? The Class of 2020 was put through one of the hardest transitions of our lives. God and faith were questioned. Why us? We may never know the answer. We do know God held us close through all of it. Even when we were tired, devastated, unmotivated, and not looking to God, He was there guiding us to the finish line. This experience has stripped us to our cores, but God has provided endurance that we can take with us through any situation. We will look back on this time and have greater trust in God—the God who brought us *out* of the trials, not *into* them. We will look back and realize how much strength is actually inside of us when we feel we have none left. We had strength even at our weakest, and only God could do that for us.

"But you are a chosen people, a royal priesthood, a holy nation, God's special possession, that you may declare the praises of him who called you out of darkness into his wonderful light. Once you were not a people, but now you are the people of God; once you had not received mercy, but now you have received mercy."—1 Peter 2:9-10 NIV

Seth Pearson, Erial, NJ, USA
Recent college graduate in Studio Art

STORY 23
SIMPLE JOYS

It's spring and our beautiful jacarandas are in bloom—very fragrant. Doves are nesting in our front porch. We work more or less part time and take care of the house and yard. I'm working at my new endeavor— selling insurance. With all the uncertainty around us, more than ever before, people want health and life insurance. My wife, Carolyn, and I also continue to call our real estate clientele, new and old, and together we show homes and write offers.

This is our dance, and it hasn't changed much since the start of the pandemic. We're online more than ever. YouTube is about the only way to have church. We actually "attend" two or three services on a Sunday and mid-week Bible studies via Zoom. Groceries are ordered online and delivered to our front porch. We like that new normal! We even exercise in front of the TV, as the gym is closed. In fact, we are connecting with friends and family even more than before the quarantine.

Nevertheless, the very real threat of catching this nasty virus casts a long shadow. We stay hydrated, take zinc and vitamin D, exercise, and get plenty of sleep. Our best defense, though, is a positive outlook and a sense of gratitude. We cultivate that in numerous ways by taking time to reflect, connecting with God during quiet time, reading the Scriptures, and sharing simple joys with kindred folk. FaceTiming with the children and grandchildren is also a great joy.

We live day by day, not always knowing what lies ahead. We may be in the wilderness, but He is with us, and the promised land lies ahead!

"The steadfast love of the Lord never ceases; his mercies never come to an end; they are new every morning; great is your faithfulness."—Lamentations 3:22-23 ESV

Bert and Carolyn Jimenez, St. Petersburg, FL, USA
Real Estate/Sales Agents and Insurance Agent

STORY 24
AN OPEN DOOR

"What are you trying to tell me, Lord?" I prayed. "What should I do?" I tried to reach out to people through numerous avenues, but the heavens were like brass. Nothing I tried was working.

As a minister of the gospel, I'm usually traveling and am rarely home. I spend my time talking to people, visiting stores or malls looking for opportunities to be around others and start a conversation.

But this global pandemic had changed life as I knew it. I had gone from having freedom of movement to self-quarantine. Spending time with others had changed to social distancing. I became seriously stressed.

The prophet Jeremiah declared, "For I know the plans I have for you" (Jer. 29:11 NIV). Although God was addressing His people, Israel, through Jeremiah, we know that "all Scripture . . . is profitable" (2 Tim. 3:16 NKJV).

At this point I began to notice an increase in text messages, emails, and letters. Each one contained questions from people frantically wanting answers. Many were scared. Others were sure COVID-19 was a fulfillment of prophecy and a punishment from God. Still others had questions about the Lord, the Bible, and the life-transforming gospel. My Lord was gently correcting me because I had missed His plan—the one He had ordained before this forced isolation began.

The Lord was opening a great door to share the Word, despite social separation. He revealed that nothing hinders the message of the cross, even though His methods may not be what we expect.

I had never envisioned this type of ministry at the outset of the virus—but God did! I'm so humbled by His great faithfulness and amazing patience.

"'For my thoughts are not your thoughts, neither are your ways my ways,' declares the Lord. 'As the heavens are higher than the earth, so are my ways higher than your ways and my thoughts than your thoughts.'"— Isaiah 55:8–9 NIV

Tom Simcox, Ewing, NJ, USA
Church Ministries Representative, Bible teacher

STORY 25
MORNING MEETING

With his dad out of the picture and his mom at work all day, my fourth-grade student had to do his own school work, plus help his little brother.

Since our school has been shut down, we have had to change to online learning, something that doesn't come easy to my students. Most are left alone to their own devices. I reach out, call parents, make lessons doable in thirty minutes or less, and I still have low participation. So, I pray for my students! I pray for their families! I pray for their minds to stay active and for them to know God.

To encourage and engage my students, I decided to have a "Morning Meeting" every day with both of my classes. Many joined in at first, but then the numbers dwindled. I prayed and asked God to send the ones who needed me or needed someone to talk to. I have about five students who consistently show up. We talk of school and books and joys and sorrows! Everyday my faithful five show up, and we are able to talk about God in public school!

God brought another "child-in-need" to our door during this time of isolation, a young woman coming out of a shelter for battered women. We first met at work and she shared with me some of her story. A month later, when it was time to leave the shelter, we asked her to stay with us. She didn't want to be a burden, but finally, through tears on Mother's Day, she asked if she could accept our invitation.

Her life has been difficult and she does not know Jesus, but she will before she leaves. I have prayed and asked God to send me the people He needs me to minister to, and He has! God, open their eyes to see you! Give me words to breathe into their lives. God, show us the way!

"Truly I tell you, whatever you did for one of the least of these brothers and sisters of mine, you did for me."—Matthew 25:40 NIV

Susan Owen, Bradenton, FL, USA
Teacher, wife, and mother

STORY 26
TIME OF FEAR

Every day we deal with a shadow of fear that cripples each person that walks through our doors. I have been a healthcare professional for many years. It is normal to see heavy foot traffic coming into our clinic to be evaluated by a medical professional. But this current health crisis has brought tangible changes to our work environment. Because of COVID-19, life at work is anything but normal. The phones ring off the hook with endless questions and concerns. You can hear the fear in their voices.

It is apparent that everyone has different reactions and that their emotions play out in individual ways. Some are on the brink of tears, others frustrated, but most have some level of anxiety. And on top of this, our staff members are required to come to the clinic and work in this environment, despite their own personal, emotional distress and anxiety.

God's Word has given me gentle reminders that provide me some perspective in this crisis. I know that my God is in control. Through all of this, it is important for us to lean on Him, be honest about our emotions, and believe that the peace He provides is greater than any other source.

"Do not be anxious about anything, but in every situation, by prayer and petition, with thanksgiving, present your requests to God. And the peace of God, which transcends all understanding, will guard your hearts and your minds in Christ Jesus."—Philippians 4:6-7 NIV

Noel Abraham, Queens, NY, USA
Medical Operations

"God is our refuge and strength, an ever-present help in trouble. Therefore, we will not fear, though the earth give way and the mountains fall into the heart of the sea . . ." Psalm 46:1-2 NIV

'Til the Storm Passes By

In the dark of the midnight have I oft hid my face;
While the storm howls above me, and there's no hiding place;
'Mid the crash of the thunder, Precious Lord, hear my cry;
"Keep me safe 'til the storm passes by."

'Til the storm passes over, 'til the thunder sounds no more;
'Til the clouds roll forever from the sky,
Hold me fast, let me stand in the hollow of Thy hand;
Keep me safe 'til the storm passes by.

(Mosie Lister, 1958)

"You have been a refuge for the poor,
a refuge for the needy in their distress,
a shelter from the storm and a shade from the heat.
For the breath of the ruthless is like a
storm driving against a wall and
like the heat of the desert."
Isaiah 25:4 NIV

STORY 27
GOD'S LOVINGKINDNESS

Driving home, I was in tears. I tried to tell myself to get over it, but the tears kept coming.

Last week I was able to go to my daughter's home and sit briefly in her garden. My youngest grandchild usually sits on my lap telling me what she's been up to while giving me sloppy kisses. This time we had to practice social distancing. I didn't realize how hard it was going to be to not give or receive hugs from my children and grandchildren. My teenage grandson even expressed to his father how weird it felt not to be able to hug me goodbye.

I tried to remind myself how grateful I should be to see them from a distance. Finally, I allowed myself to lament over the loss of closeness. We as believers know how to cry out to the Lord. Michael Card writes in his book, *A Sacred Sorrow: Reaching Out to God in the Lost Language of Lament*, ". . .lament is not a path *to* worship, but the path *of* worship." Later in the book, Card pens, ". . .[God's worth] is the central issue of worship: What is God worth? In fact, the first primitive form of the word was 'worth-ship.'"

Let us use these days of staying at home to worship the Creator of the universe. Our hope is that through lamenting the world's chaos, confusion, lostness, and hopelessness, God's lovingkindness will be shown throughout the world. Who knows if we might witness, as in the days of Moses, the deliverance of His people? "I have surely seen the affliction of my people who are in Egypt, and have heard their groaning, and I have come down to deliver them . . ." (Acts 7:34 ESV).

"Be patient, therefore, brothers, until the coming of the Lord. See how the farmer waits for the precious fruit of the earth, being patient about it, until it receives the early and the late rains. You also, be patient. Establish your hearts, for the coming of the Lord is at hand."—James 5:7-8 ESV

Gretchen T., Fredericksburg, VA, USA
Widow, mother of three, grandmother of six

STORY 28
DOG IN THE BED

During the quarantine, I think the one who struggled the most in my family was my husky pup, Link. (Well, I guess he's not technically a puppy, but all dogs are puppies. Right?) Huskies are very active, so we usually take him to daycare twice a week. We also visit extended family a couple times a week where he can play with other dogs. Then the quarantine happened. No daycare. No hanging out with family. Our poor dog was trapped inside the house—with us!

I think that not being able to play with other dogs was making him a little more stressed than usual. Then came the night of a huge rainstorm. The lightning was bright and the thunder was loud. My dog, who doesn't spook easily, was terrified! Though he doesn't usually sleep in our bed, this sixty-pound dog jumped up and squeezed between my husband and me. He ended up in my arms under the blanket with his head snuggled up on my husband. Finally he could settle down and fall asleep.

The next morning, as I was retelling the story to my mom, I was reminded that God does the same for us. During a time when we are all a little more stressed than usual, there are things that can bring us to our breaking point. 2 Corinthians 1:3-4 ESV says, "Blessed be the God and Father of our Lord Jesus Christ, the Father of mercies and God of all comfort . . ."

When we hit our breaking point, God is there to envelop us in His arms. We can rest our heads on His shoulder and be comforted. In His presence, we can let go of our stress and find rest. Once we are comforted, we can use the peace that God has given us to comfort others.

"Blessed be the God and Father of our Lord Jesus Christ, the Father of mercies and God of all comfort, who comforts us in all our affliction, so that we may be able to comfort those who are in any affliction, with the comfort with which we ourselves are comforted by God."—2 Corinthians 1:3-4 ESV

Rachel Ferguson, Hamilton, OH, USA
Wife, restaurant training director, and mom of "Link the husky"

STORY 29
WHERE DOES YOUR STRENGTH LIE?

As I wheeled a cart full of books, whiteboards, and markers out to my car, my mind swarmed with ideas. I was determined to turn my daily lessons and time spent with my students into an enriching remote learning experience. My type A, planner-self went into overdrive creating video recordings and Google documents.

I kept hearing people complain of boredom while binging on TV shows. I struggled with quite the opposite. My already busy life had just become more chaotic. No more alone time during my thirty-minute drive to and from school. No more separation of "teacher hat" and "mom hat." I now simultaneously held Zoom calls with my students, while getting blasted with nerf bullets by my sons.

This quarantine brought me to my knees in a new way. I needed God's peace and strength now more than ever. How could teaching my own sons possibly be harder than teaching twenty-two children? I began to doubt my abilities and my calling to be a teacher. Slowly I let the voice of the enemy creep into my mind.

After a particularly rough day, I began to intentionally look for the lesson He was teaching me. God so graciously reminded me that He uses our struggles to refine us and edify others. Maybe God is allowing this struggle so that I can, in turn, extend grace to my students and their parents. It is likely that they are trying to juggle helping their child and doing their own work from home, just like me.

God has reminded me that I cannot teach at home in my own strength. It is by *His* power that I can carry out the task before me. In the miracle told in John 6:1-15, Jesus fed 5,000 people after a little boy offered all that he had, and his gift was multiplied! I need to offer my gift of teaching to God, for Him to multiply His anointing in my life.

Lord, help me to keep my eyes on You—and not the storm—as I continue to navigate through this new season. Amen.

"' . . . Not by might nor by power, but by my Spirit,' says the Lord Almighty."—Zechariah 4:6 NIV

Elizabeth Jackson, Medford Lakes, NJ, USA
Teacher and mother of two

STORY 30
TURNING TO PRAISE

I didn't really feel like rejoicing as I dropped off my wife at the emergency room after what was now her fifth day struggling to breathe. It was the loneliest I have ever felt. This was worse than three days earlier when I myself walked through the same doors. Thankfully, I was released only hours later, but this was different. I had now seen so many cases where loved ones had been dropped off never to be seen in this life again. Based on the rules set out by health professionals, no visitors were allowed. Because her location was a Wi-Fi black spot, there was limited communication. Due to my wife gasping for air, we couldn't talk.

We were both struggling with COVID-19. I'd like to say my first port of call was to converse with God. The truth is, the first place I went was into my own head. Let's just say, it wasn't pretty. Despair probably isn't a strong enough word. After a while, my focus turned to the only One who could actually help me, but even my prayers were depressing. That is, until I read Habakkuk, who was also in a time of despair. But he had a different response—he turned to praise!

Even though the circumstances were dire, that did not mean God had changed. God was still good, and as I began to acknowledge that, my perspective started to change. God had been with me in the past, and He would be with me through this. I'd like to say that my focus remained this way for the next seven days as my wife remained in the hospital. Honestly, I fluctuated between hopeful and hopeless. I was learning the hard way, like Habakkuk, to rejoice despite my circumstances.

"Fig trees may not grow figs, and there may be no grapes on the vines.
There may be no olives growing and no food growing in the fields.
There may be no sheep in the pens and no cattle in the barns.
But I will still be glad in the LORD; I will rejoice in God my Savior.

The Lord GOD is my strength. He makes me like a deer that does not stumble
so I can walk on the steep mountains."—Habakkuk 3:17-19 ICB

Evan Peet, Queens, NY, USA
New York City senior pastor

Update: We are happy to report that Evan's wife made a full recovery!

STORY 31
CAMERA HOG

"Are you going to read us a story, Nonna?" That's how the Zoom session began as I was about to read a book to my two grandsons in Florida, Ryon, age seven, and Carson, age three.

I responded to Carson's question with a yes, and his little face lit up with a smile. I started reading the book, trying to get each of them to interact with me. We had a good time talking about the story as I unfolded the secret flaps in the book which revealed once-hidden colorful pictures.

Afterward, Ryon started to chat with me about his day as he is very outgoing and loves to talk. In fact, he talked for quite a while—so much so that Carson started to get jealous. Vying for my attention, the little one put his face right up to the camera, blocking his brother from view, and proceeded to tell me about his new toy.

By the time the Zoom session was coming to an end, Ryon started pouting and was slowly walking away.

"What's wrong, Ryon?" I asked.

"I guess you don't want to hear the rest of my story," he said sadly. "So just forget it."

I felt bad, but after some coaxing, Ryon finally came back and finished his story. Although I love both boys the same, I can only listen to one of them at a time. I'm glad God isn't like that. Especially in this time of trouble when many are crying out to Him at the same time, I know that He listens to everyone's prayers and has the ability to give each one of us His undivided attention whenever we call upon Him.

We don't have to "jump in front of the camera" to try and get His attention, or sadly walk away thinking that He doesn't care about us. God listens to us and loves us even more than I can love my grandsons. And that's saying a lot.

"You have searched me, LORD, and you know me. You know when I sit and when I rise; you perceive my thoughts from afar. You discern my going out and my lying down; you are familiar with all my ways. Before a word is on my tongue you, LORD, know it completely."—Psalm 139:1-4 NIV

Bonnie R. Pearson, Erial, NJ, USA
Author, *Hope When the World Shut Down*

STORY 32
GOD IS IN CONTROL

It was March 30. As I lifted the shades and looked out my windows, I discovered yet another rainy, depressing day of home confinement. Although we were still in the early days of many weeks of quarantine, life around me had come to a screeching halt. I was already feeling the weight of a growing knot of fear in my heart and mind. I feared a deadly disease, yes, but I mostly feared the unknown. I feared for my loved ones. I was also dealing with the ever-nagging question: Why was God allowing all of this to happen?

In that moment, looking beyond the gray skies, I saw the beauty of bright yellow daffodils and forsythia in bloom. This beautiful sight reminded me once again that God is in control of this world, no matter what kind of insanity rages around us. Spring had arrived right on schedule and the earth was once again awakening to the renewal of life. Birds were singing and gathering materials to build their nests. They showed no signs of fear or worry.

My heart was immediately lifted, and I took a moment to thank the Lord for the beauty all around me. It was a precious reminder that while this current health crisis came as a huge surprise to me, nothing is a surprise to God. He knows all things, and ultimately, controls all things. He promises in His Word that He will never leave, forsake, or abandon us in our times of need.

Today, I am praying that you, too, will be encouraged by the knowledge that no matter what man or Satan may try to accomplish, God remains in control. He is still on the throne! In these troubling and chaotic times, let's choose to place our trust wholly in the One who gives us hope. He is the very author and creator of order, joy, peace, and beauty!

Thank you, heavenly Father, for the precious promise of Your gifts of peace and hope when we put our trust in You, even in the very midst of the raging storm.

"May the God of hope fill you with all joy and peace as you trust in Him."—Romans 15:13 NIV

Katrina Butts, Lancaster, PA, USA
Wife, homemaker, lover of God, music, and writing

STORY 33
MAMA BEAR

The year 2020 has been an odd one, to say the least. New things have entered our culture: songs about being bored in the house, quarantine haircut-fail videos, jokes about the world-infamous "Tiger King," and survival homeschooling.

As a mother of three young kids, my "mama bear" instincts have kicked in. I have not allowed them to touch a door handle, let alone pick up a Cinnamon Life cereal box, before taking a Lysol wipe to it. Confusion starts to set in about what is the *right* thing to do during this unprecedented time. As an avid rule-follower, I make sure to walk with the arrows at the store and stay six feet away from everyone. But then, over at the fruit section, a lady with an attitude confidently coughs all over the cucumbers! And the internet is no help with the supposed whistle-blower documentary, "Plandemic," and angry conspiracy Facebook posts.

Through it all, I have had moments of frustration and confusion with what to do and how to protect my family. What I have settled on in the middle of all this confusion is this: people are scared. Scared people cope in different ways. Some hunker down and stock up. Some deny the situation is even real. Some align themselves with "experts" to give themselves a false sense of hierarchy above the common "sheep."

But God's Word says in 1 Corinthians 3:18 NLT, "Stop deceiving yourselves. If you think you are wise by this world's standards, you need to become a fool to be truly wise." We can't know what is really *right* and *true* in a global pandemic. But we *can* know that only God knows all things, Christ holds all things together, and the Holy Spirit convicts the heart. At the end of the day, it doesn't matter who is right. What matters is that we rely on the truth of God's Word, be Christ's servants, and be stewards of the gospel.

"This is how one should regard us, as servants of Christ and stewards of the mysteries of God. Moreover, it is required of stewards that they be found faithful."—1 Corinthians 4:1-2 ESV

Erin Roten, Alliance, OH, USA
Wife, musician, and mother of three under seven years old

STORY 34
SPRING TRAINING

Colorful images of players in red and white under a canopy of tropical palm trees is something I will never grow tired of watching. It's spring training season with the Phillies in Clearwater, Florida, and the crowd is cheering!

After our week of excitement and fun, I noticed Cindy, my "Phillies Buddy," wiping down our seats on the airplane with hand sanitizer. It was the beginning of March, the start of the pandemic, but at that point I wasn't concerned that it was going to be a big deal.

I couldn't wait to give spring training gifts to my grandchildren when I returned home. What a shock when my own children were hesitant to give my grandchildren their souvenirs. I was hurt. When I called my doctor to ask about the virus, she suggested a two-week self-quarantine because of my travels.

However, just as my quarantine was over, the statewide stay-at-home order was announced. I felt like I had been home by myself forever.

During this time, I was careful to limit my time watching the news as it was difficult to handle stories about COVID-19. I was also trying to cope with the disappointment of not being able to visit my grandchildren or my mother, who was at a long-term care facility. I wondered if I'd ever see her again here on earth. My mom has been the biggest influence in my life and is the one who taught me the importance of reading my Bible daily.

I had already been reading through the Bible, but it greatly intensified under the stay-at-home order. As a retired Social Studies teacher, I love history and journaling, including research, verse-by-verse applications, and writing down my thoughts. I have filled almost fourteen notebooks from the Old and New Testaments! I found unexpected blessings as I was able to spend even more time in God's Word.

My time of quarantine began with baseball spring training, but ended by training me to spend even more time in the Word. While there is a certain loneliness to my situation, I am never alone, as I am never without Jesus, my Lord and Savior.

"Behold, God is my salvation; I will trust, and will not be afraid; for the Lord God is my strength and my song, and he has become my salvation."—Isaiah 12:2 ESV

Georgia Stanfill, West Deptford, NJ, USA
Retired teacher, grandmother, and Phillies fan

STORY 35

WHEN I DIDN'T THINK I COULD—JESUS DID!

"God, You are going to have to help me, because I am scared."

I was having my first home birth in the middle of a pandemic. It seemed my only choice as the hospital was restricting visitors, and my husband couldn't be in the delivery room. The dangers of contracting COVID-19 in the hospital were too great. What if my precious newborn got sick? So, at a week and a half overdue, even though I was completely in denial, I was giving birth—right now—at home!

The midwives and my husband, Tony, set up the mini hospital in our living room. I thought of all the women who had done this before, even in the pandemic a hundred years ago, and felt at peace. Every contraction brought my baby closer to his new, uncertain world. Less than thirty minutes later, on April 11, precious Judah made his entrance. It was a surreal and heavenly moment. The peacefulness into which he was born did not match what was happening in the world, but God had kept little Judah and Mommy safe and sound.

We had planned and prayed for this baby. God made it clear that He wanted this precious addition to our family, but the pregnancy was a difficult one. I wrestled with guilt and anxiety. Then in March, I learned that two of my three boys would have to be schooled at home. At thirty-seven weeks pregnant, I became even more anxious and needed God to show me what to do.

Then God sent me Joanna Davis, a certified midwife with medical knowledge, professionalism, and a beautiful spirit. I considered a home birth knowing it would come with risks, but did they outweigh the dangers of a hospital birth during a crisis? Joanna set my heart at ease, so I made my decision. God showed up in the midst of my crisis and gave me clear direction with peace.

And so I birthed at home in the middle of a global pandemic. In that moment, with my family safe at home, and a fresh baby on my chest, I felt that all was right with the world.

"Because you have made the Lord your dwelling place—the Most High, who is my refuge—no evil shall be allowed to befall you, no plague come near your tent."—Psalm 91:9-10 ESV

Rebekah Postlewait, Parkersburg, WV, USA
Wife, mom of four, and now "home-birther"

STORY 36
BEAUTY FOR ASHES

Living "Down Under" has presented ongoing challenges for our family during this past summer's longest-ever drought and worst bushfires in our nation's history, but worse was to follow.

Immediately after the destructive flames were quenched, weary survivors rummaged through the ashes of burnt homes. Hundreds in so many communities had perished, and the nation was reeling from financial loss. Then COVID-19 arrived! Total lockdowns were enforced, and the country came to a standstill!

In Isaiah 61, God promises to give us *beauty for ashes*. From the literal ashes in which so many beloved friends found themselves, we discovered that we, too, were not exempt. Our *ashes* were metaphorical, but very real to us. After the start of an unprecedented family crisis, we suddenly lost our opportunities to serve in the beautiful, fulfilling ministries we had enjoyed for more than fifty years in combined service for the Lord Jesus (the Messiah). The ministries that had taken us far and wide were gone! What were we to do? Pray!

Then *beauty for ashes* began to appear. Three examples will suffice.

First, an interstate couple contacted us, asking if we would mentor and disciple them personally, via IT media.

Second, we were burdened to help friends in Israel who had lost jobs because of the COVID-19 crisis. God enabled us (and others) to share with them in their need.

Third, an eighteen-year-old university student texted me to ask if I would talk to him about Jesus. He had been thinking about this for the past two years since he and his parents had moved from living across the lobby from us in our condo complex. We shared the Scriptures with my young enquiring friend, and he prayed to receive the Lord.

The *ashes* have now gone, dissipated by the wondrous beauty of His presence and power! What a privilege to journey with this sovereign Lord of all circumstances! He really does give *beauty for ashes* in ways often hitherto unknown. May you continue to find this to be so today!

"The Spirit of the Lord God is upon Me . . . to console those who mourn in Zion, to give them *beauty for ashes*, the oil of joy for mourning, the garment of praise for the spirit of heaviness; that they may be called trees of righteousness, the planting of the Lord, that He may be glorified."—Isaiah 61:1-3 NKJV

Deane James Woods, Th.D., Castle Hill, Sydney, Australia
Ministry representative, pastor-teacher, father of four, and grandfather of eight

STORY 37
SCRATCHING MY HEAD

"Huh?" I said, scratching my head. I was told to work through Friday and then work remotely from home. We were now under the COVD-19 quarantine.

"We don't know when we will be back. Take anything from your desk that you might need."

It was so fast. I thought working from home and not commuting would be so much better. Less stress, less pressure. This was great! Or was it?

Looking back to the beginning of the lockdown, my first thoughts were of what it would be like for me and my husband. He would be doing the same job, but work remotely. We set up our offices and settled into working at home.

As the weeks of the pandemic went by, many questions came up:

- They say to be socially distant! What would that require?
- We had to wear surgical masks. What? Is this a new fashion statement?
- Stay six feet apart from one another. Difficult? We'll see.
- No touching! This is tough for a parent and grandparent, and others too.
- Don't gather in groups! What about church?

The myriad of emotions we have felt are widespread and shared by our families, church friends, and work associates. We all have feelings of being separate, lonely, confused, and yes, angry. We realize, even more, the importance of our relationships.

So what do we do about it? We can go to the source for answers. Scripture gives us a powerful message that I claim daily in verses from

Colossians 4. We are instructed to pray constantly, with vigilance and thankfulness, and to pray for opportunities to tell others about the truth of the gospel of Jesus Christ.

As I pray for others, I am reminded of the many prayer warriors that are active in my life. The power and miracles of their prayers have been humbling. They are a blessing and I am thankful for them all!

"Continue steadfastly in prayer, being watchful in it with thanksgiving. At the same time, pray also for us, that God may open to us a door for the word, to declare the mystery of Christ, on account of which I am in prison."—Colossians 4:2-3 ESV

Kim Clark, Stratford, NJ, USA
Administrative assistant, mom, and grandmom

STORY 38
SIDELINED

"Put me in, coach, put me in!"

I was one of the many healthcare workers furloughed during the coronavirus pandemic. I was placed on the bench while eagerly screaming to be put in the action. I didn't want to go back to work only for the money. I *desperately* wanted to get back to work for the same reason I went into the healthcare field—to help people. I even volunteered my services to the state government offering COVID-19 assistance, potentially uprooting myself 1000 miles away with no financial incentive.

How was I going to help from the sideline? By sitting on the bench. I stayed home. My "job" during my furlough was to keep the COVID-19 numbers low. I haven't even been to a store since the night the NBA suspended the basketball season.

From home, I was able to cheer from the sidelines. I advocated for the physical therapy profession regarding issues of Telehealth services and Student Professionals' Clinical Education. I checked up on my healthcare colleagues, many of which are only a year out of school and already experiencing burnout. I took care of myself physically and mentally so I could go back to work stronger than I left.

Even though I went to school to be a healthcare professional and have a desire to help people, I realized helping people doesn't always mean helping patients. It can be neighbors, colleagues, strangers, friends, and even myself.

Amid my furlough, I found purpose in being "non-essential." That being said, I'm very grateful to be returning to work today . . . mask and all.

"When I am afraid, I put my trust in you."—Psalm 56:3 NIV

Kristine Sindoni, Bartlett, TN, USA
Physical therapist

STORY 39
GOOD GIFTS

Life was hard enough when, unexpectedly, one of our two vehicles quit working. We still had to get everyone to their designated locations throughout the week. My husband and I both work full-time jobs. We have two children, one in daycare and one in elementary school, each school 45 minutes away. That was our lives for nine months. Getting everyone to their destinations with one car.

Our schedules were hectic and exhausting! We were trying hard to save for a new vehicle, yet every time we would get a substantial amount saved, something would happen to drain our savings. We had been praying for a new vehicle. Our families had been praying we would find a new vehicle. At some point, I think we kind of gave up hope. It didn't seem like it was ever going to happen, especially with the COVID-19 pandemic shutting down my job.

One morning, things changed for us. My husband's aunt and uncle had a friend who was selling a used van for a ridiculously low price. He was even willing to set up a payment plan that worked with our budget. The van had only had one owner, and he had kept it in immaculate condition. It was almost too good to be true! The deal of a lifetime just fell into our laps! The van was an unexpected blessing and solved several of our transportation problems.

My hope in my heavenly Father and His provisions has been renewed. It was exciting to be on the receiving end of such a big blessing!

"Every good and perfect gift is from above, coming down from the Father of the heavenly lights, who does not change like shifting shadows."—James 1:17 NIV

Elizabeth P., Leesburg, FL, USA
Wife, mother, and restaurant server

STORY 40

ONE DAY AT A TIME

"I'm sorry, I don't think your husband is going to make it."

I felt helpless. I was supposed to accept that my husband was going to die, but I wasn't going to be able to say goodbye!

Life with Charlie living in a nursing home was hard before the pandemic, but we had settled into a nice routine. I'd see him every day. I helped him play solitaire, made sure his laundry was perfect, fixed him snacks, changed him, and tucked him into bed before heading home. I loved watching him joyfully singing along with his favorite song, "One Day at a Time Sweet Jesus."

That all changed when they closed the nursing home to visitors. Weeks passed and I wasn't able to contact Charlie. During that time, I only had one phone call with him, but my dear Charlie had begun withering away. I could barely hear him, and I'm not sure that he could hear me.

Charlie was a believer so I wasn't worried where he would go if he passed away. But I worried that he might be in pain, or that he didn't understand why I never came to see him.

"I'm sorry, I don't think your husband is going to make it," the voice said on the other side of the phone. I did get to have one final phone call. I could see and hear Charlie, but I didn't know if he could see me. It was heart-wrenching. He was trying to mouth the words "I love you."

They said Charlie passed away peacefully, but I felt no comfort as I had longed to be there for him.

Charlie was buried at a veteran's cemetery, and I wasn't allowed to go. I still feel deep grief, but church friends have been very supportive. I don't know how people without the Lord can survive. Although I miss him and sometimes feel I am drowning in despair, I take comfort in knowing that one day I'll see Charlie again. And because of our faith in Jesus, we will dwell in the house of the Lord forever.

"Surely goodness and mercy shall follow me all the days of my life, and I shall dwell in the house of the LORD forever."—Psalm 23:6 ESV

Cindy James, Mount Laurel, NJ, USA
Retired teacher, business owner, and social worker

STORY 41

MASTER GARDENER

I've always loved flowers and trees. I grew up in Florida, which is the Spanish word for "flowery," and then moved to New Jersey, the Garden State.

Outside my new home, there was a beautiful holly tree in my neighbor's yard. Its copious branches filled the entire view behind my house, spilling across my fence. The tree soared high above and beyond my roofline, gently swaying back and forth in the ocean breeze. I loved having this spirited, living privacy fence.

With green prickly foliage, it provided a cheerful home for grey squirrels. Over the years I watched them build their nests and raise their tiny babies. The juicy red berries supplied ample food for seasonal birds. Flocks of robins, cardinals and blue jays would come for their wintry feasts on the small fruit. When the snows came, my eyes were always glued to my back windows, captivated with childlike joy. I felt blessed to have the quintessential Christmas tree in my backyard.

But the peaceful bliss the tree afforded me was quickly snatched away at the most inopportune time. One day, during the pandemic, I heard a whirring sound coming from behind the house. I looked out my back window and discovered that my neighbor had used a chainsaw to cut down the beloved tree!

I was shocked and dismayed. What would happen to the birds and squirrels and the beauty it added to my backyard? Soon I saw my neighbor with a tilling machine, cultivating the soil. He explained that he had always wanted to have a green lawn surrounded by flower and vegetable gardens. The holly tree had prevented sunlight from passing through. Nothing could grow as long as that impenetrable shade remained. I began to understand that he had a master plan, which included the removal of that tree.

So it is that God has a master plan for the garden of my life. In order for Him to till and cultivate me, He has to cut away the trees that keep me from growing in the "Son."

"Every branch in me that does not bear fruit he takes away, and every branch that does bear fruit he prunes, that it may bear more fruit."—John 15:2 ESV

Mariano Jose Jimenez, Ventnor City, NJ, USA
Musician

STORY 42
ETERNITY TO ETERNITY

"Are you scared?" my boss queried as he popped inside the doorframe of my office, swallowing a bite of lunch.

"Afraid?"

I recalled emails and messages foreshadowing the coming pandemic.

"No," I added, "but we need to be prepared, to think ahead. At the very least, the virus has potential to impact enrollment. This is peak enrollment season."

It is February 28, 2020. Even though Japan is on the other side of the world, the sudden shuttering of Japanese educational institutions signaled the dangers of this virus that had been wreaking havoc in countries that are close to China. As a teacher, I am concerned.

I remember that in January, the virus piqued my interest and I began to see red flags. It was an unknown virus spreading imperceptibly—and no one was immune to it. There was uncertainty about how it spread, and death was overwhelming local hospitals. Even scientists were alarmed about the severe symptoms, even in those who recover. Wuhan, China shuts down. The rest of the world begins to take notice as travel strengthens the spread, moving it outside of China, and now inevitably to North America.

God, in His wisdom, had already protected us. In July 2019, my husband had travelled to Wuhan, China, for work, and announced the possibility of moving there. I did my research, as I have done many times before, when my husband talked about relocating. Thankfully, the move didn't happen.

Nothing surprises God. He is omniscient! God already knows. He is already in our future. He sees our grief and our joy. He sees it all. We are mere mortals, dependent upon almighty God. The Bible is replete with examples of imperfect humans relying on God before, throughout, and after calamity.

Am I afraid? At minimum, these months challenge our resiliency, producing confusion, anger, and death. However, God remains immutable and He knows the end of our narratives. When I look to Him and contemplate the fact that He sees everything, I am able to rely on His grace and truly trust. My perspective is transformed and truth reigns within. Nothing in our mortal lives surprises God. He is in control from eternity to eternity.

"Lord, You have been our refuge in every generation. Before the mountains were born, before You gave birth to the earth and the world, from eternity to eternity, You are God."—Psalm 90:1-2 HCSB

Deborah de Oliveira, Horseheads, NY, USA
Wife, mother of four, and teacher

STORY 43
CHANGED IN AN INSTANT

As a newly married woman, so many things had already changed. I wasn't sure how I would handle the challenge of the coronavirus. My husband is a pastor, and quickly after we were married, he accepted a position as a NextGen Pastor in New York City. Being married has been exciting, but we had never moved away from our families, especially to an unfamiliar city. I took comfort in knowing that, if we needed to, we could visit our parents in South Jersey.

After a few weeks, I found a job at a dental office and I was finally able to slip into a routine. Not only were things going well for me, but my husband's ministries were thriving, and we were excited for what was to come. Little did we know everything was about to change again.

A short month into my new position, people were cancelling their appointments due to the coronavirus. I was frustrated. This was getting in the way of the normalcy I needed after what seemed like a crazy beginning of our marriage.

Very quickly, my office was forced to close just as my husband and I became sick with COVID-19. We knew right away we needed to fight the virus and be quarantined for fourteen days. Once we recovered, I thought things would return to normal, but they only got worse. Though we had already had the virus, going out for necessities was stressful and scary.

I realize now how blessed we were that we didn't have serious health issues. Others were not as fortunate. We were feeling better, but the rest of America was struggling. It was going to be a while before I worked again.

Getting back into a routine is important for me, but I am thankful for the extra time to read my Bible. I keep returning to Hebrews 13:8, "Jesus

Christ is the same yesterday and today and forever." I never imagined beginning my marriage in the epicenter of a pandemic, but I learned that while God can change our lives in an instant, He will always stay the same.

"Your faithfulness endures to all generations."—Psalm 119:90 ESV

Teresa Gollihue, Freeport, NY, USA
Wife and partner in NextGen ministry

STORY 44

SPLIT PEA SOUP

Being a cooking enthusiast, I always enjoy making large quantities of food. One day during the pandemic, I had a craving for cozy comfort food. I started on a big batch of one of my favorites—split pea soup! As I was chopping the onions, celery and carrots, I began missing my kids and my grandkids scattered around the country. I began missing the days when we were all together and I could cook for them.

My kids live in North Carolina, California, and Philadelphia, so I wasn't able to visit them in person. I could, however, FaceTime them, and I was grateful. As I stirred the simmering soup, I began turning my thoughts outward. I envisioned people with needs all around me—overworked healthcare workers, first responders, those with COVID-19, and those who had lost their jobs due to the virus. Suddenly I had an idea. I began spooning my split pea soup into containers and gave it out to some of my neighbors. Seeing that there was so much more to give, I called a local ministry that serves drug addicts, the homeless, and the downtrodden. While they were not able to feed anyone in large groups, they knew of several families in need and sent a van to pick up eight quarts of soup from my home.

My joy was full. Although I wasn't able to share a meal with my family, the Lord allowed me to share His love with others in the form of split pea soup.

". . .being like-minded, having the same love, being one in spirit and of one mind. Do nothing out of selfish ambition or vain conceit. Rather, in humility value others above yourselves, not looking to your own interests but each of you to the interests of the others. In your relationships with one another, have the same mindset as Christ Jesus."—Philippians 2:2-5 NIV

Marietta M., Westville, NJ, USA
Mother of four, grandmother of three, and social services worker

*"In the same way, let your light shine before others,
that they may see your good deeds and glorify your
Father in heaven."—Matthew 5:16 NIV*

Marietta's Split Pea Soup

2 quarts water
1 lb. bag dried split peas
3 tablespoons powdered ham base
½ cup chopped onion
salt (to taste)
black pepper (to taste)
1 cup chopped carrots (cut into 1/2" pieces)
1 cup chopped celery (cut into 1/2" pieces)
1-1½ cups smoked ham (1/2" pieces)

Bring peas & water to a boil in a large pot for 2 minutes. Turn off heat
& let it rest for 1 hour. Stir in powdered ham base, onion, salt, and
pepper and bring to a boil. Reduce heat to low, cover and cook for 1
hour, or until peas are tender.

Cut carrots, celery, and smoked ham into 1/2" pieces and add to pot.
Bring to a boil, then simmer with the lid on for about 45 minutes or
until vegetables are tender. Serves 6-8.

STORY 45
BATTLE OF THE MIND

My mind started bouncing off the walls with regrets from the past—the would've beens and could've beens. I worried about what would happen in the future. The past ten years my life had been dedicated to the art that gave me freedom of creativity—tattooing. Tattooing had occupied most of my time and was my personal escape from reality. It also made me feel like I had value and was contributing to society. Not to mention, it was my source of income and sustainability.

Then the pandemic came and boom! Non-essential workers were ordered to shut down their businesses to protect themselves and their clients. I thought my shop would only be closed for two weeks, but it lasted months! I had no idea how to fill the giant hole in my life that had been filled with the art of tattooing.

It affected my thoughts, my mood, and eventually my actions—and it just got worse. Walking with the Lord is a daily fight and the battle raged on in my mind. The pandemic had caused a lot of fear, anxiety and worry. Living through the time of quarantine also revealed the lazy side of me—mentally, spiritually and physically. These three areas are connected and affect both our thoughts and behaviors.

I prayed and asked God for help and He reminded me of a drawing I had sketched last year. This specific piece of artwork woke me up and reminded me that I should let God take control of my thoughts, and that I should stay vigilant through challenging times.

Fear, panic, and worry are not from the Lord. Where your mind goes, the body will follow. Watch your thought patterns. If you are in the middle of a spiritual battle, you are not alone, and you don't fight alone. Stay blessed and never give up.

". . . Be strong and courageous. Do not be afraid; do not be discouraged, for the Lord your God will be with you wherever you go."—Joshua 1:9 NIV

Ned De Leon, Ventnor City, NJ, USA
Tattoo artist

STORY 46

GROUNDHOG DAY

I wake up, go downstairs, eat breakfast, and bring coffee into the living room. While sitting on the couch and looking out the bay window, I begin to look at the never-ending to-do list I began at the start of the quarantine.

My mind races to all the things I could try to tackle that day. Will it be writing a story? Will it be writing a new song or practicing an instrument? Will it be writing a card or note to someone? Or maybe I should organize a closet?

Then I reach down into the basket for my prayer journal and Bible. Looking through the prayer requests, I quickly pray for a couple of them. Then I thumb through the Bible and read a verse or two. I'm distracted by a new idea for a story or a song, and before I know it, I'm typing away on my computer or sending an email.

I hear my phone beep, reminding me of yet another cancelled event on my calendar. I think, wow, I should really take advantage of my added free time and spend more time in Bible study and prayer.

In the movie *Groundhog Day*, the main character is perpetually trapped in the same day. He finally figures out after several years of going through the same routine of the same day, that each day is a fresh start—a new chance to get it right!

So, perhaps tomorrow when I wake up, go downstairs, eat breakfast, bring coffee into the living room, sit on the couch, and look out the bay window, I'll get it right. Maybe I'll spend more time in prayer and put more thought into my Bible reading. And hopefully the routine will spill into a regular habit, even long after the pandemic is over.

"But his delight is in the law of the Lord, and on his law he meditates day and night."—Psalm 1:2 ESV

Bonnie R. Pearson, Erial, NJ, USA
Author, *Hope When the World Shut Down*

STORY 47
LETTING GO OF PLANS

We make plans for our lives—weddings, vacations, parties, get-togethers, birthdays, and retirement. Then something unexpected happens, like COVID-19, and everything changes.

In December 2019, my boss, who is seventy-one years old, updated our computers and bought new equipment. I felt secure in the fact that she wasn't going to retire any time soon. I am almost sixty-three and wanted to work at least the next two to three years before retiring.

During this time, I was happily anticipating the birth of my grandson. I planned my vacation time excited to help my daughter with the baby while she was in the hospital, or possibly when they first came home.

But things didn't turn out as I expected. No one could have predicted the onset of the coronavirus and its effects on the world around us. Today, as we are quarantined and shut down, I find myself at home barely working and partially on unemployment.

I struggle that I wasn't able to be there for my daughter. I found myself having to work on the morning she had her baby as I could not refuse work while on unemployment. My life is filled with uncertainty, not knowing if I'm going to have a job to go back to when this is over. I don't know if my boss's business will be able to recover.

Through all of this, I have learned that even as we make our plans, we never know when life will change in an instant. The pandemic has given us the opportunity to put our lives in perspective and not take each other for granted. I may not know what to expect, but I take comfort in knowing that God is in control. May His will be done!

"Come now, you who say, 'Today or tomorrow we will go to such and such a city, spend a year there, buy and sell, and make a profit'; whereas you do not know what will happen tomorrow. For what is your life? It is even a vapor that appears and then vanishes away."—James 4:13-14 NKJV

Anastasia G., Berlin, NJ, USA
Transcriber, mother of three, grandmother of five

STORY 48
SERVING OTHERS

While planning our Easter dinner, I was saddened that my grocery list was much shorter than usual. Instead of cooking a big ham dinner for my entire extended family, this year's dinner would only include me, my husband, and our children.

My name is Colleen. My husband, Jon, and I are a homeschooling family that live in West Virginia with our five children: Rebekah, age seven; Daniel, six; Noah, five; Job, three; Seth, one; and baby girl Chloe, due in July. For the most part, life has remained the same as we face this pandemic. My husband has an essential job as a nurse, I've always been a stay-at-home mom, and our children are homeschooled.

During this time, God has given our family opportunities to serve others. After preparing our own Easter dinner, we decided to take a couple of plates over to my husband's elderly aunt and uncle. When it was time to deliver their dinners, my two oldest children wanted to come along. After a nice visit, outside and at a proper distance, my children talked about how much they enjoyed the opportunity to serve. I could hear the joy in their voices. The impressions of helping those in need will remain with them forever.

Although we experience times of blessing, we are also called to go through challenges. A few of my family members in New Jersey ended up sick with COVID-19. Everyone had a mild case, but my children were very concerned. They reminded us every day to pray for them. They have now all fully recovered and we are thankful for God's mercy.

Whatever unique situation we find ourselves in, we can always trust God to be our refuge. We can fully rest in Him. Psalm 91 has been such a comfort to me during these uncertain days.

"He who dwells in the secret place of the Most High
Shall abide under the shadow of the Almighty.
I will say of the Lord, 'He is my refuge and my fortress;
My God, in Him I will trust.'
Surely He shall deliver you from the snare of the fowler
And from the perilous pestilence.
He shall cover you with his feathers,
And under His wings you shall take refuge;
His truth shall be your shield and buckler."—Psalm 91:1-4 NKJV

Colleen S., Wellsburg, WV, USA
Mother of five children, and one on the way

"When I was a boy and I would see scary things in the news, my mother would say to me, 'Look for the helpers. You will always find people who are helping.'"

- Fred Rogers
(Fred Rogers Productions. Used by permission)

STORY 49
STRENGTH FROM GOD

"We can't get tested!" Being a young man at the start of a global pandemic, I knew I wasn't going to be first in line for COVID-19 testing. But I was so sick. The health department left me on hold and never returned our calls.

I had already been through a hectic ten months. I had gotten engaged, planned a wedding, moved twice, gotten married, and accepted a pastoral position in New York. So many positive things were happening. My wife and I found an apartment and moved to Freeport, NY, beginning our adventure working as NextGen pastors. We were just starting to get to know the youth of the church, when suddenly the coronavirus made its entrance. We knew everything was about to come to a stop.

This was when I woke up not feeling well, and neither did my wife. We weren't worried. We didn't know anyone with the virus. But just as we were coming down with "something," we found that our senior pastor, his wife, three of their children, and other friends had all tested positive. Same symptoms, same everything. We soon realized we had been repeatedly exposed to many people with COVID-19 within just a short few days. I knew what that meant.

As services and ministries went online, I wondered how I could make new plans and learn new technology when I felt like I couldn't function. My wife was doing much better, but my condition was bad from the beginning. Every day I felt worse to the point where it was difficult to breathe. Hot showers made it worse.

While this was happening, my online ministries began. I had to develop infrastructures, programming, and the basic DNA of what online ministry would look like for people ages three to twenty-two.

I had learned to depend on God before, and He brought me through this as well. He has restored my health and enabled me to do His work.

God has so much in store for us after this time of shutdown. Embrace the opportunity to fall deeper in love with Jesus and to grow in His strength.

"He gives strength to the weary and increases the power of the weak."— Isaiah 40:29 NIV

Kevin Gollihue, Freeport, NY, USA
Pastor in Queens, New York City

STORY 50
FLOWERS

How often in the Scriptures are we admonished to "fear not" or "be not afraid?" There are moments I lie in bed in the morning filled with fear, but not the fear of getting sick. I am prepared for that. My fears have been much darker and more nefarious—fears the enemy tries to use to torture me.

It's tempting to believe our lives are over, that we won't ever truly live again. We believe we will never again experience the good gifts we have been given in the past. These are the times we're tempted to sink down inside ourselves and embrace despair. I have fallen into this temptation.

One such dark day, I was given the simple gift of the flowers in the field outside my bedroom window. They were beautiful! God had reminded me again of His goodness. "I lift up my eyes to the mountains, where does my help come from? My help comes from the Lord, the Maker of heaven and earth" (Ps. 121:1-2 NIV). Our minds can be renewed, but we must make the choice of what we allow to come in.

Nothing in your life is a surprise to God. He chose for you to live where you live. He gifted you and placed you specifically "for such a time as this" (Est. 4:14 ESV). He has already mapped out a path before you and prepared good works for you to do. Rest in the beauty of His sovereignty over both the number of your days, and the purposes He has for you.

He still gives us flowers!

"For we are God's workmanship, created in Christ Jesus to do good works, which God has prepared in advance as our way of life."—Ephesians 2:10 ESV

Betsy Clark, High Point, NC, USA
Mother of four

STORY 51
ALL FOR GOD'S GLORY

Being a stay-at-home mom with a potty-training toddler, while your husband is out to sea for months, isn't an easy lifestyle. Especially not during a pandemic. Sometimes I go through my day like a robot. Other days I want to cry. Some days I feel like I have it together.

It's easy to feel that all I do is cook and clean. Leaving my child alone for a break means finding the precious toilet paper you finally found at the store strung up all over the house. I have noticed that on the days I struggle, it is because I have forgotten my purpose. God says to glorify Him in everything I do. When I clear my mind and focus on why I clean, why I cook, and why I teach my child, I am able to have peace. When I focus on the *why*, I am able to do housework while belting out worship songs and dancing with my child.

There are times when I feel the isolation the most. Times when I start comparing myself to others I see on social media and how they are serving. How can I serve others when I am at home with my toddler? Do I even have a purpose? That's when, in my quiet time with God, He whispers, "Alisha, you are not like everyone else. Your gifts and personality are unique. Your situation is unique. I am always using you, so let me continue."

I want to encourage you to open your heart, ears, and eyes to see how God has called you to serve in your situation. And don't forget the *why* in the midst of your daily routine. You are not alone, and you have a purpose—to worship God. "Lord, help us worship You in all we do. Amen."

"Therefore, whether you eat or drink, or whatever you do, do all for the glory of God."—1 Corinthians 10:31 ESV

Alisha Pearson, Strafford, MO, USA
Child of God and privileged to be a stay-at-home mom

STORY 52
PAY IT FORWARD

I reached into the mailbox and pulled out a small white letter. As I started back to the house, my curiosity got the best of me. I tore open the envelope even before I got back inside. To my delight, carefully wrapped in white paper, was five hundred dollars in cash! There was no return address. Though I sat and analyzed the handwriting, I couldn't figure out who had sent that welcomed gift.

Years ago, when we owned our home, life hit us hard. We didn't have the money to pay the mortgage. We prayed and prayed, and about a week later, God answered our prayer with that mysterious surprise!

Fast forward to the pandemic. Although money was a little tight for our family, I knew there were many families who had it much worse. Never forgetting what that anonymous gift meant to me, I wanted to make sure I was doing my part to help others. There are so many creative ways to encourage people: ordering their groceries, paying utility bills, cooking or baking for them, or even sharing food from your own garden. Wouldn't it be fun to watch someone go out to their mailbox and tear open a little white envelope with a nice surprise in it?

I still smile and thank God when I think about that special answer to my prayer that prompts me to pay it forward.

"And do not forget to do good and to share with others, for with such sacrifices God is pleased."—Hebrews 13:16 NIV

Ruth Racke, Salem, OR, USA
Schoolteacher

STORY 53
DESIGNER JEANS

During the pandemic we had to cut back on our spending. That meant I couldn't always have the take-out I craved, or that item I "just had to have" on the internet. I had to learn to be content with the simpler things of life. It made me think of a modern parable I had written years ago.

"Disgusting! I wouldn't be caught dead wearing these!" muttered Kathy. She held up the offending garment for inspection—designer jeans with metallic designs on the back pockets. Then she remembered how she ended up in this thrift shop in the first place. She was window shopping. Her mood was overcast as she ruminated on "unanswered prayers." Feeling a divine nudge, she walked into the store.

From experience, she understood that at these times, the Holy Spirit wanted to show her something. As she stared at the designer jeans, a powerful memory came back to her. She was fourteen, living on the family farm. She shuddered as she remembered pleading with her parents, "If I don't get a pair of designer jeans, I will die! I can't go to my new school dressed in hand-me-downs. No one will want to be my friend!" Her parents were sympathetic but couldn't help. Later, weeping, she pleaded with God for the grand miracle of owning a pair of designer jeans. They never came.

Now, years later, Kathy looked lovingly at the jeans before her, finally realizing that God had answered her real request—to be accepted and have friends. Instead of designer jeans, God had arranged for something far better—a youth group at her church. With fondness, she smiled, thinking of the happy memories of her church and the miracle of the friends that God had provided.

I know that God still works small miracles every day. There is a certain peace to knowing that God is in charge. Even when finances are tight, He will give me what is best for my life, even if it's not the designer jeans I had hoped for.

"Call to me and I will answer you, and will tell you great and hidden things that you have not known."—Jeremiah 33:3 ESV

Dwight J. Racke, Salem, OR, USA
Defense Contractor to the Oregon National Guard

STORY 54
SOUND MIND

It was a night I will always remember, even twenty-five years later. I was behind a platform curtain listening to an eighty-four-year-old legend share his testimony about how God had taken his wicked life and transformed it into something new. He had been a foreign government spy and had been used to expose many hundreds of thousands of people to harm. Through His grace, God changed his heart and used him to defy this regime and expose their deeds. I remember being so captivated by his story that I momentarily forgot my own anxieties about having to speak after him.

Following his testimony, he came backstage and saw that I was anxious. Somewhat short in stature, he proceeded to grab my tie, pull me down, and whisper into my ear, "Dean, I notice you are anxious to talk in front of the crowd. Embrace your anxiety, because you have two choices: either you rely on yourself, or you rely on God." As he let go of my tie, he said, "Relying on God is a gift that will change your life," and he walked away.

In this time of pandemic, don't deny your anxieties. You can't put them away as if they don't exist. We all have fear, including some of the great leaders in the Bible. Moses doubted his ability to speak and lead. Jeremiah and David were threatened by their enemies. Timothy had to be exhorted by Paul to continue in the ministry. Imagine the day when we can all sit around together in Heaven and share our stories.

In 2 Timothy, Paul reminded young Timothy not to let his anxieties get the best of him. Paul saw his heart, gifts, and passion, and recognized that coaching Timothy would further God's mission into the next generation. Paul encouraged Timothy to lead through his anxieties with power, love and a sound mind.

God is always trustworthy and is your greatest weapon against anxiety. Place your trust in the powerful presence of God. He will never let you down. No matter what anxiety you might be facing, it is no match for the Lord your God.

"For God has not given us a spirit of fear, but of power and of love and of a sound mind."—2 Timothy 1:7 NKJV

Dean Bult, Ventnor City, NJ, USA
CEO of Bult and Associates and pastor

STORY 55
SO MUCH TO DO

Who would have thought I'd be taking walks every day with my busy teenage son, a junior in high school? The exercise, fresh air, and sunlight were beneficial to our health, especially during those days of isolation from the world around us.

Through the weeks of quarantine, I was pleasantly surprised at the things God allowed me to do. On May Day, I crafted handmade cones for several of my neighbors. I filled them with individually-wrapped chocolate chip, peanut butter, and Oreo cookies, and some fresh flowers from the shrubs in my backyard. It was a fun way to bless and encourage these neighbors as springtime began to blossom.

Because my son enjoys film production, with his help, I had the opportunity to film several YouTube videos. I recorded a video-reading of two illustrated Easter stories for children. I also recorded a craft video to show young girls how to make Mother's Day cones with flowers, and a heart tulip Mother's Day card. My daughter and I had a good time together filming an instructional video on how to have a simple, lovely tea for two, encouraging other women to have one in their homes.

We should always remember that God is in control as He reigns in Heaven above. Jesus is our Immanuel—God with us. Jesus is with us in this boat, and He will calm the storm with His healing hand. We are all in this together. May God bless you and fill you with living hope.

"Be still, and know that I am God; I will be exalted among the nations, I will be exalted in the earth!"—Psalm 46:10 NIV

Vivian Sielaff, Pembroke Pines, FL, USA
Substitute teacher, Bible club mentor, widow of eighteen years, and mother of two

"Be good to yourself. You don't have to be rich to feel rich in spirit. Drink your tea from your most beautiful china cup as it will help lift your spirits as you sit down and relax about your day. Perhaps it may be even just a few minutes to have a quiet time with God to just pray and reflect on your day—just you and Him in dialogue of prayer as you sip from your teacup. Invite a friend to join you and savor a sweet time of fellowship . . ."

- Vivian Sielaff
viviansielaff.wordpress.com/2014/03/19/
tea-anyone-garden-tea-party/.

STORY 56
LITTLE THINGS

Just as we were turning the clocks forward one hour in March, the country entered a twilight zone. The world was thrust into chaos due to the pandemic. This was the start of uncertainty, sickness, and death. For many, this became a time-out, a time to rest, a time to dwell on life and repent of sin.

For me personally, I decided it would be best to establish a daily routine. I began my day talking to God, reading the Bible, and enjoying my much-needed quiet time with God. I kept in touch daily with my neighbors, especially those who were elderly or ill. I tried to encourage those who seemed depressed, lonely, or afraid.

Because I now work only one day a week, I am able to spend more time with my daughter. We take walks together, and although we are social distancing, I cherish our times together as a precious gift.

Before the pandemic, there were times I was so busy that I forgot to appreciate nature. Living "down the shore," I have started to watch the sunrise and take walks on the beach at sunset. In the middle of the night, I listen to the ocean waves crashing onto the shore. The rhythm of the sea lulls me to sleep at night. In the morning, I wake to the sound of chirping birds.

My boyfriend and I are also learning not to take each other for granted. We now verbally say "I love you" each day and intentionally spend time together. We realize how blessed we are to have each other. In the "twilight zone," I am reminded once again to appreciate the little things in life.

"By the word of the LORD the heavens were made, and by the breath of his mouth all their host. He gathers the waters of the sea as a heap; he puts the deeps in storehouses. Let all the earth fear the LORD; let all the inhabitants of the world stand in awe of him!"—Psalm 33:6-8 ESV

Leesa Toscano, Ventnor City, NJ, USA
Actor, poet, writer, and case manager

STORY 57
SAFE AND SECURE

My mother has been bedridden for seventeen months now. I guess for some, life has changed drastically during this time of COVID-19—for me, not as much. My life has already been scaled back and focused here at home. I have learned rich lessons. Sitting with my mom is not wasted time. Talking with my grandchildren is time well invested. Extra time with the Lord and in His Word has eternal weight.

When things change, as they seem to daily, I am reminded of Psalm 107 and the truth that God's steadfast love endures forever. When I was in Bible college, forty years ago, I used to take my Bible out to a huge rock that was in the woods on campus. I would climb up on that rock and feel safe and secure. I knew the Lord was my rock and my strong foundation. Today I am reminded of that same truth!

Things may be changing in our world at a rapid pace, but the steadfast love of the Lord endures forever! He is still the rock of ages and we need to put our trust in Him. Change can be good if the result turns our eyes to the unchanging One.

"Oh give thanks to the Lord, for He is good, for His steadfast love endures forever! Let the redeemed of the Lord say so, whom He has redeemed from trouble, and gathered in from the lands, from the east and from the west, from the north and from the south."—Psalm 107:1-3 ESV

Joanne Callahan, Laurel Springs, NJ, USA
Wife, mother, Nana, and caregiver for Mom

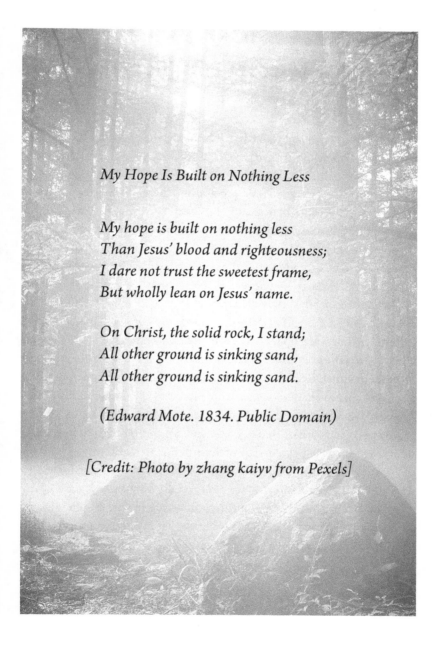

My Hope Is Built on Nothing Less

My hope is built on nothing less
Than Jesus' blood and righteousness;
I dare not trust the sweetest frame,
But wholly lean on Jesus' name.

On Christ, the solid rock, I stand;
All other ground is sinking sand,
All other ground is sinking sand.

(Edward Mote. 1834. Public Domain)

[Credit: Photo by zhang kaiyv from Pexels]

STORY 58
BACK TO BASICS

Years ago, I took on the task of distributing thousands of books intended for Russian Jewish émigrés in the United States. An organization I knew of needed someone to take the books off their hands as soon as possible. The alternative appeared to be grinding them up for recycling—I couldn't bear the thought of that! I said yes and even built an extension to a shed on my property to help hold all the books. Distributing the books became a monumental challenge. Although I live in Virginia, I found a grocery store in Brooklyn that allowed me to place free books in their shop. I travel often, so whenever I make a trip to New York, I replenish the store with a fresh supply of literature.

Then came the COVID-19 shutdown. My trips to New York were halted. I had to come up with a new plan of action to give out the books. I decided to take the time to research and find people who might benefit from them, much like I did in my early days of ministry. It was tedious, but I was able to send books to people in cities like New York and Los Angeles. While the number of books sent out was on a smaller scale, I prayed that each of these books would encourage the hearts of those who received them with the message of hope in the Messiah.

This whole experience has shown me that it's all right for me to slow down. I am able to use creativity and whatever tools are at my disposal to minister, even if it means going back to the old-school ways of doing things. God takes what we have that is old and transforms it into something new!

"See, I am doing a new thing! Now it springs up; do you not perceive it?"—Isaiah 43:19 NIV

Jim Melnick, Fredericksburg, VA, USA
President, Friends of Russian Jewry, Inc.

STORY 59
SOMETHING LOVELY

When the quarantine began, my husband and I were unnerved. We both struggled with anxiety on normal days. Suddenly we were consumed with a bunch of irregular days with no end in sight. Coming home from a walk, my husband and I noticed how horrible the garden in front of our rented house looked. It was full of rocks, dead plants, and a bush that grew wildly out of control.

Thinking this might be a good project for us, we contacted our landlord to work with him to improve the garden. My husband toiled to remove the rocks that prevented anything beautiful from growing. It was hard and laborious, but the moment my husband began removing the rocks, his anxiety automatically dropped.

After the rocks had been taken away, the bush had been trimmed, and the dead plants removed, we spread new, fresh soil into the garden and planted beautiful flowers. Our garden project had finally reached its goal. We officially turned an eyesore into something lovely.

While putting in the work, my husband and I realized we were not much different than the abandoned garden. We had become full of fear and anxieties which allowed for nothing to grow. It's difficult to learn to trust God with your worries, but as you slowly hand those things over to Him, your anxiety lessens and the load you have been struggling under becomes lighter.

It may be hard, and at times even painful, but when we truly learn to be vulnerable with God, He can shine through us. We can become another beautiful flower in His garden. I challenge you to be vulnerable with God so that He may change you and make you into a flower radiating hope to others.

"A voice says, 'Cry out.' And I said, 'What shall I cry?' 'All people are like grass, and all their faithfulness is like the flowers of the field.'"—Isaiah 40:6 NIV

Alisha Yowell, Stillwater, MN, USA
Wife, author, and freelance writer

STORY 60

HOPE AT THE END OF THE TUNNEL

Surgery was over for my husband and he was resting comfortably. In just a few days he would be coming home, and we could start getting back to normal again—or so I thought. Not long after my husband recovered, I began having health issues. That year became an endless blur of problems, one after the other. It seemed like a never-ending tunnel. But we gradually saw light and the hope of full recovery.

Sometimes the coronavirus quarantine also feels like an endless tunnel. But when heartache seems overwhelming, we can take comfort from people in the Bible who also hung in there through difficult situations.

Noah preached repentance for a hundred years while his neighbors were indifferent to his words. Job stayed true to God after everything was taken away from him. And ultimately, Jesus was beaten, spit upon, ridiculed, and crucified for nothing He had done. Being sinless, only Jesus could pay for our sins. He could have spared Himself and stayed with the Father, but He humbly obeyed and sacrificed Himself, enduring terrible suffering for us.

Because of His death on the cross and His resurrection, we also have a certainty of resurrection. We can persevere knowing that in a very short time, all of our heartache, suffering and sickness will be over. We will be forever with Him. Our lives here are only a grain of sand compared to eternity.

When the world peels away like an onion, and all the comforts of this life are taken away, in the center there will be God. He is the light and hope at the end of the tunnel.

"I consider that our present sufferings are not worth comparing with the glory that will be revealed in us."—Romans 8:18 NIV

Marlene Rosenthal, Groveland, FL, USA
Wife, mother, and "Grammy" to six grandchildren
and four great-grandchildren

"May the God of hope fill you with all joy and peace as you trust in him, so that you may overflow with hope by the power of the Holy Spirit."
—Romans 15:13 NIV

STORY 61
SPIRITUAL ARMOR

Some mornings during quarantine, I wake up thinking that perhaps it's all just a surreal dream. But the other day when I got into my car to run errands, I was eerily reminded that it is not a dream.

Pulling into the gas station, the cars at the pump were sparse, even though gas was at an all-time low of $1.85! I never get used to the sign on the supermarket door that reads, "No admission without a mask." The song "Follow the Yellow Brick Road" takes on a whole new meaning as I follow the social distancing tape and then am greeted by a masked clerk behind a plexiglass barrier. *Am I playing a part in the last scene from E.T.?* I remember thinking how ridiculous that part of the movie was. It seemed so over-exaggerated with everyone running around in "space suits."

Repeatedly, I'm tempted to think that I don't need to arm myself with a mask, hand sanitizer, gloves, and social distancing. I wonder, is this really real? I can't even see these tiny invisible germs, yet they are undeniably wreaking havoc throughout the world.

Then a sobering thought occurs to me. I sometimes think the same thing about putting on the armor of God. Because I can't physically see the enemy, I'm tempted to think that he's not real—until I see the results of the havoc he can cause in my life.

So yes, for now I won't run out the door without being armed with my mask and hand sanitizer. But even after this crazy quarantine is over, I'll have a new reminder not to run out the door without my spiritual armor.

"Put on the full armor of God, so that you can take your stand against the devil's schemes."—Ephesians 6:11 NIV

Bonnie R. Pearson, Erial, NJ, USA
Author, *Hope When the World Shut Down*

STORY 62
SET APART FOR GOD

There have been times in my life when I needed to be more like Martha in Luke 10, serving and ministering to people. But this season of quarantine has been a time I've needed to be more like Mary, sitting at the Lord's feet spending time just listening to Him.

I've been enjoying reading through Genesis, Exodus, Leviticus, Joshua, Judges and John. Today I decided to change things up a little and read something from one of the Psalms. I smiled as I opened to Psalm 4 and read, "Answer me when I call to you, my righteous God. Give me relief from my distress; have mercy on me and hear my prayer. How long will you people turn my glory into shame? How long will you love delusions and seek false gods? Know that the Lord has set apart his faithful servant for himself; the Lord hears when I call to him" (Ps. 4:1-3 NIV).

The dictionary defines *quarantine*, "to isolate from normal relations or communication or to detain or exclude." I love the phrase, "the Lord has set apart the godly for Himself" (Ps. 4:3 ESV). *To set apart* means "to select [something] for a specific purpose ... to separate or isolate." Both words are similar in some ways. COVID-19 has caused us to be isolated, set apart, or separated from others. I love that the purpose of being set apart in Psalm 4 is that God has set us apart for Himself! Amen! That means we have a specific purpose! In Psalm 4, David is reminding us that we are a people set apart for God's glory—not to be mixed in with the world.

"But know that the LORD has set apart the godly for himself; the LORD hears when I call to him."—Psalms 4:3 ESV

Joanne Callahan, Laurel Springs, NJ, USA
Wife, mother, Nana, and caregiver

STORY 63
RENEWED VIGOR

This pandemic took me by surprise. Instead of visiting my friends, I began to phone them. Instead of inviting them to events, I wrote letters and sent reading materials. I found I had more time to pray for them while learning to cast my burdens upon the Lord.

My life already had been filled with major adjustments. I had moved from Montreal, Canada, to Bordeaux, France, to serve the Jewish people here. I speak fluent French, but I still had to get used to the culture changes. I was homesick. To help me through, I decided to learn biblical Hebrew. I love biblical languages and have been studying Hebrew to use in my discussions with my Jewish friends.

A heavy burden I carry is the veil of blindness on the eyes of these dear souls. When I challenged one of them recently to read the Bible for herself, she said, "I can't read or understand the Bible without the help of commentaries from our sages." And I am saddened at the roots of bitterness against the lost sheep of Israel everywhere, especially here in Europe. This can be a very heavy burden after thirty years of it. It seems to grow heavier as the years go by, causing my strength to diminish.

In my study of Isaiah 40:31, I gathered a better understanding of what the verb *chalaph* means: being renewed, exchanging my failing strength for His mighty strength, waiting for Him to fill me with wisdom instead of relying on my own. This realization caused the weariness to vanish and renewed vigor ensued.

God has taught me to let the ravens feed me like they did Elijah, who was weary and discouraged after heavy battles with his enemies. God provided streams in the desert. Yes, our Savior is very present in times of trouble. His everlasting arms are there to catch us when we fall, just like the eagle is ready to catch her young when they learn to fly.

"He gives strength to the weary, and to him who lacks might He increases power. Though youths grow weary and tired, and vigorous young men stumble badly, yet those who wait for the LORD will gain new strength; they will mount up with wings like eagles, they will run and not get tired, they will walk and not become weary."—Isaiah 40:29-31 NASB

Ginette Albert, Vichy, France
Domestic Engineer

STORY 64
SWEET SIXTEEN

Ever since I was a little girl, I dreamed of having a huge sweet sixteen birthday party. I still remember my friend planning hers in seventh grade and thought, "Wow, that's such a long time away!" Finally, the year came when I would turn sixteen. I started planning my party in February, even though my birthday wasn't until May. I was going to invite a lot of people, play games, listen to music, and have an awesome sweet sixteen like I had always dreamed of.

I made a folder on my phone with the guest list, games, and song ideas. I couldn't wait! Then, around mid-March, we were told we were going to do online schooling because of the quarantine. We had to bring all our books home for what we thought would only be a week or two.

Most of us really thought we'd be going back. Who would've thought we'd be out for the rest of the year? I was so upset when I heard we weren't going back to school. I never said a proper goodbye to all my friends. Our yearbooks remained unsigned, and the spring musical was cancelled. This was a big disappointment because I had gotten a pretty good part this year. More and more events started to be cancelled. My mom reminded me not to dwell on the things we lost, but to think about what we still have, like family.

My birthday rolled around pretty quickly. I was still sad that I couldn't have my party, but my mom surprised me. My friend came to visit and I had a drive-by birthday party with a lot of my family and friends! As I watched each car pass by my house filled with people that cared about me, I realized how blessed I am. Social distancing rules were starting to lighten up a little so my aunt, uncle, and cousins came over for a bonfire.

It wasn't how I expected my birthday to be, but it was still an awesome day that I will never forget!

"Finally, brothers and sisters, whatever is true, whatever is noble, whatever is right, whatever is pure, whatever is lovely, whatever is admirable, if anything is excellent or praiseworthy, think about such things."—Philippians 4:8 NIV

Laura Barrett, Stratford, NJ, USA
High school student

STORY 65
EMBRACE THE STRUGGLE

Three years ago, I left my home in New York to go to college in Dallas, Texas. I was going to miss New York, but the one thing I would especially miss was home-cooked meals. By my second year, I was hooked on this place called Chick-fil-A. It was the only place I would eat. After going home for a visit, I saw my grandma and the first thing she said was "Andrew, you're fat now?" Everyone was laughing because of how blunt my grandmother is, but it was true. I was getting chubby. Chick-fil-A was once the Lord's food, but now it was the devil!

I decided I was going to diet and workout at the gym. Once I started, though, I was feeling so sore. In the beginning, I hated it and didn't understand why my muscles were hurting so badly. I asked a friend who told me that when you work out, it's a constant cycle of literally tearing your muscles, and then rebuilding them through eating and resting. This is how your muscles grow and get larger and stronger. Once I understood this, I began to embrace being sore and loved the results it gave. I was looking and feeling great, but most of all, I developed self-confidence.

This concept of growth was harder to apply during this time of the coronavirus and quarantine. A lot of us fell into the trap of praying to make the problem go away. We wanted to get back to our normal lives and treat this time as if life were on pause. I believe, though, that God doesn't want us to take this time for granted. As we struggle with this season of shutdown, the question is not why we have these struggles, but what are we going to do when the struggles come.

Rejoice in these challenges because, just like when we work out, resistance is an opportunity for growth. Take this time to develop an intimate relationship with God, read His word, and talk to Him. That way, when storms come, you can recognize it as an opportunity to grow.

"We can rejoice, too, when we run into problems and trials, for we know that they help us develop endurance. And endurance develops strength of character, and character strengthens our confident hope of salvation. And this hope will not lead to disappointment. For we know how dearly God loves us, because he has given us the Holy Spirit to fill our hearts with his love."—Romans 5:3-5 NLT

Andrew Gravagna, New York City, NY, USA
Long Island, New York pastor

STORY 66
LESSONS FROM ADVERSITY

Last week my wife, Joanne, was speaking with a young woman who had brain cancer. She said to her, "The Bible says that 'All things work together for good to them that love God . . .' (Rom. 8:28 KJV). What good has come from this?" She replied that it had strengthened her relationship with God and had given her a new outlook to appreciate all the little things in life! You couldn't ask for better lessons of the heart.

In Ecclesiastes, Solomon compares adversity with prosperity. Which one is better? Most people would probably say prosperity.

It's not that Solomon doesn't think we should enjoy life. He tells us that prosperity is a gift from God. But which one gives us better instruction for life? Adversity. It's not that our hearts feel better when we are going through times of sadness, it's that our hearts are able to learn more through hardship. God has a purpose for both prosperity and adversity. "When times are good, be happy; but when times are bad, consider this: God has made the one as well as the other" (Eccles. 7:14 NIV).

In the midst of a lockdown from the coronavirus, we are definitely under adversity, but God has a purpose in our hard times. He has things for us to take to heart, things for us to consider, that would elude us in good times.

This lockdown has given me a small glimpse of what persecuted believers around the world might be facing all the time. They can't meet for church and must be very careful what they say. They have to "cover" their mouths to keep from offending, never knowing when the authorities may be watching. They can be isolated from family and restricted from living normal lives. Praise God that our restrictions are only temporary.

"Better to go to the house of mourning than to go to the house of feasting, for that is the end of all men; and the living will take it to heart. Sorrow is better than laughter, for by a sad countenance the heart is made better."— Ecclesiastes 7:2-3 NKJV

James Callahan, Laurel Springs, NJ, USA
Husband, father, and missionary homes director

STORY 67
NEEDLE IN A HAYSTACK

"Please, please. I know you're busy, but can you review my application next?" The woman at the other end of the phone sounded desperate!

During the shutdown, I continued to work as a social services provider. Although I was sympathetic toward this woman's plight, I was also aware of the high volume of applications that came in each day. The amount of need is immeasurable. So I gave her my usual response. I told her that applications are processed in the order they are received. I explained that with our limited staff, I could not give her a timeline and assured her that we process them as quickly as we can. Our agency had received 4,500 applications in just six weeks. Finding this woman's specific application would not be easy. It would be like finding a needle in a haystack.

After hanging up with her, I went back to my task of giving out applications to workers for processing. Much to my surprise, hers was the next one on the pile! It was assigned, processed, and reviewed in the next hour. She had her benefits the very next day! She called back to thank me and said that I was her angel.

God knew of her need and used me to meet it at that specific time. I sat back in awe of how great God is, and how He uses people like me to help others in their greatest time of need.

"And this same God who takes care of me will supply all your needs from his glorious riches, which have been given to us in Christ Jesus."—Philippians 4:19 NLT

Brenda Lucas, Clementon, NJ, USA
Civil servant, wife, mother of four, Grandma to five, foster grandma, and ladies' Bible teacher

A vessel of honor, I'm longing to be.
As clay to the potter, may I be to thee.
You may have to break down resistance at times.
But Lord don't stop molding and shaping my life.

- Gary S. Paxton

STORY 68
THAT'S OUR GOD!

Sickness. Loss. Pain. Isolation. Loneliness. Financial struggles. Uncertainty. Fear. Doubt. This season of COVID-19 has been full of hardship for many. I've experienced all of this, if not firsthand, then certainly second. For me, in addition to all these, I have faced the challenges of cancelled wedding plans, my parents' sudden divorce, multiple transitions in life, and a daily "mental boxing match" with depression and anxiety.

The words of the Psalmist certainly resonate with me when he laments in Psalm 94:19 that his cares are many. My cares are many in this season. At times, there are so many that I don't know if I can bear it. Maybe yours are as well. I am so glad it doesn't end there for the Psalmist, and it doesn't end there for me or you.

The Psalmist continues in the second half of the verse, saying, "your consolations cheer my soul" (Ps. 94:19 ESV). Consolations of comfort, solace, compassion, sympathy, and love. Consolations that can't be found anywhere else like they are found in our Heavenly Father. Consolations that have brought me through the most worrisome times and the darkest of nights. That's our God!

If you've been in the church for any period of time, you will likely have heard the phrase, "God works in mysterious ways." To me, this concept is a mysterious thing. How can God swap all my worries and hardship for such compassion and solace? I may not understand it, but I am grateful and blessed that He does! He did that for the Psalmist, He's done that for me, and He can certainly do that for you. It's all available by His grace and love.

I want to encourage you today, whatever season in life this finds you in, and whatever today's worries may be, to look to God. Allow Him to bring consolation in the midst of your calamity, anxiety, uncertainty, or any trying circumstance. Look towards Him, and you will find His unrivaled, unconditional, matchless consolation.

"When the cares of my heart are many, your consolations cheer my soul."—Psalm 94:19 ESV

Levi Gaska, Rockaway Beach, NY, USA
Student Ministries Pastor, House on the Rock Church

STORY 69
SMALL BLESSINGS

"Hello, God. What are you doing today?" Each morning I read the little sign on my bathroom mirror and think, *whatever it is, God, I want to be a part of it!*

How will we remember our COVID-19 days? I will remember how busy I was because God has not let me be bored. I've spent more time in His Word—hopefully listening. My day is filled with activities. I make many phone calls to check on friends and have sent so many cards that I might be keeping the U.S. Postal System in business. I have also received cards from others. They are a wonderful encouragement to me as I see them sitting on my kitchen table.

Every morning I walk with a group from my neighborhood. We are believers, so we uphold each other. Then in the afternoon, we have our "sanity" walk. By then we have cooked and cleaned too much, but we are still on God's mission.

I have been able to stay in touch with family and friends through the technology of Zoom. We have Zoom meetings for Sunday school class, birthdays, prayer ministry, book club and Wednesday night prayer meetings. Since Sunday morning worship is online, it has been easy to invite others to join, and I've become bolder!

One day God sent me "begging" for one of our ministries at church. The food pantry was running low, so He sent me off with mask and gloves to ask for donations from grocery stores. God's work has not been defeated!

I am able to see the blessings in small things. It is spring and the flowers are beautiful because I am taking the time to see them. What a blessing are the small things! While there are times of joy, like everyone, I have felt discouragement, but I know that God is my sustainer. As

Americans, we say we are "one nation under God." Please, Father, make it so—make it be so!

"So do not fear for I am with you; do not be dismayed for I am your God. I will strengthen you and help you; I will uphold you with my righteous right hand."—Isaiah 41:10 NIV

Martha W.W., Fuquay-Varina, NC, USA
Jesus follower, wife, mother, grandmother, and volunteer

STORY 70
WAITING ROOM

When was the last time you were in the waiting room? What were you waiting for? News, help, recovery . . . a miracle? Waiting is difficult.

It was about two years ago that God blessed our lives in a remarkable way with the birth of our granddaughter. Her parents gave her the name Elsie Jean. Her "Papa" calls her "Elsie Jean Beauty Queen." She is an absolute delight, but Elsie was born with a genetic translocation. Her genetic coding was all jumbled up. Elsie Jean will go through life with a completely compromised immune system and has almost died from the common cold.

One particular night, Elsie Jean was in the hospital NICU—again. It was about 3:00 a.m. and the nurse noticed her vitals dropping rapidly. We watched some of the best trauma specialists battle for her life. Three times they shocked her little body to try to compel her heart to beat. They battled for what seemed an eternity when her heart fluttered back to life. Elsie remained in a coma for nine days and in the NICU for forty days. In fact, in the first eighteen months of life, she was in the NICU for nearly 120 days.

Our family learned a lot about waiting rooms. Waiting rooms are the place we process the dark night of the soul, where we argue with God, and where we wait for the answers that are beyond our control. It is in the wait that Jesus transforms us, when He shapes and reshapes our hearts. The words of the Psalmist best captured our experience, "I wait for the Lord, my whole being waits, and in his word I put my hope . . ." (Ps. 130:5-6 NIV).

It seems that all of us are waiting for something. In the midst of a world-wide pandemic, we are waiting to get back to life as we know it. We wait to get out of our homes, rebuild our businesses, restore our relationships, celebrate our milestone moments, and simply feel normal again.

In the wait, let's learn to trust the Lord and trust His Word. He will prove himself faithful in the wait.

". . . Then you will know that I am the Lord; those who hope in me will not be disappointed."—Isaiah 49:23 NIV

Brian Pipping, Daphne, AL, USA
Christ follower, pastor, husband of one, father of seven, and grandfather of five

STORY 71
GARDEN VISITS

Suddenly, in the blink of an eye, our world changed. Churches were closed. Industries and businesses were shutting down. Airplanes were grounded. As a flight attendant, I found myself quarantined at home with no agenda.

My life had always been busy working a full-time job, being a pastor's wife, spending time with family, and watching my granddaughter. In the last several years, I've had the additional challenge of health problems. A series of downfalls and illnesses have made me feel as though I couldn't keep up.

With all the demands on me, my body grew weaker. At times I felt as though I would cry out for things to stop and yet no one heard. "They cried, but there was none to save them: even unto the LORD, but he answered them not" (Ps. 18:41 KJV).

During the quarantine, I woke up every morning and went to the garden, sitting in disbelief and sadness at what was going on around me. In time I realized that, in a strange way, my prayer had been answered. Without the noise of cars and airplanes, I could hear the birds singing. I could watch the bees as they flew from flower to flower. I was able to visit the garden and see the beauty all around me. My soul was filled with wonder.

Before this pandemic, I had felt like I was on a speeding train headed nowhere. Now it was a relief to stop and embrace the quiet, to embrace the peace. I felt myself being able to have longer conversations with God. I told Him of my fears and thanked Him for the beauty.

I encourage each one of you to find a quiet place and talk to God. It is in our quiet that we can hear Him more clearly. Embrace the quiet to hear others speak. Take in and digest the words and actions of your husband and your children. Listen and observe and you will gain a greater appreciation of the world around you.

"'For my thoughts are not your thoughts, neither are your ways my ways,' declares the Lord. 'For as the heavens are higher than the earth, so are my ways higher than your ways and my thoughts than your thoughts."—Isaiah 55:8-9 NIV

Monica Everett, Atlanta, GA, USA
Wife, mother of three with a 13-year-old in Heaven
Grandmother, pastor's wife, retired flight attendant

STORY 72
BALLET SLIPPERS

As a little girl I always dreamed of being a ballerina. Ballet dancers were always so pretty and got to wear those lacy pink tutus. But the best thing about being a ballerina was that she danced in beautiful pink ballet slippers.

Sadly, I never got to take ballet lessons. I would look on wistfully as other girls danced in recitals. As I've grown older, I still admire the women that can dance with grace, ease, and coordination.

So when I had the chance to take adult beginner ballet class, I eagerly, but cautiously, enrolled. I was self-conscious and out of shape and wondered if I could cut it. But the class was fun. Although, at my age, wearing a tutu was out of the question, I finally got to wear the beautiful pink ballet slippers!

The teacher was patient and moved at an unhurried pace, but in the studio room there was nowhere to hide. If I didn't get the footwork right, the instructor and other women were right there to see it. There were mirrors everywhere!

After several classes, the studio had to cancel the lessons. My ballet career had ended—until the pandemic hit. I reconnected with the teacher and asked if she would give us lessons online. She graciously agreed and we began virtual dance classes on Zoom. Fortunately, my webcam obstructed anyone from seeing my feet. Not even the teacher could see if I was doing the right footwork.

While using Zoom, I was able to hide my feet from the instructor, but my feet are visible to God wherever I am. Whether out on the street, or stuck at home in quarantine, God is always looking for me to have "beautiful feet," sharing the gospel any way I can. God expects us to have our dancing shoes on both "in season and out of season" (2 Tim. 4:2 NIV). How is your footwork?

"How beautiful on the mountains are the feet of those who bring good news, who proclaim peace, who bring good tidings, who proclaim salvation . . ."—Isaiah 52:7 NIV

Bonnie R. Pearson, Erial, NJ, USA
Author, *Hope When the World Shut Down*

STORY 73
NO DOUBT

My friend asked me if I am finding life more difficult and challenging during these days of coronavirus. I had to honestly answer that no, I am not. I have severe macular degeneration, but I have learned to trust in the Lord. Though my eyesight has become more and more limited, I have no doubt that the Lord is there to help me. I know everything will be okay. I go from hour to hour, day by day. Life goes on and I have nothing to fear. I don't fear walking or falling. My trust is in the Lord!

I used to be a professional interior decorator, but with my eyesight impaired, I find it very difficult to see colors and shapes. While this has been a real challenge to me, there are other challenges as well. In the past, I never had to depend on others—I could take care of things myself. I have found that even though I need others to help me with so many things, the Lord has given me opportunities to serve Him.

So, coronavirus? This is no different for me than trusting the Lord with all my daily challenges. I have no doubt that He is with me and helping me all day, every day.

"For we walk by faith, not by sight."—2 Corinthians 5:7 ESV

Gloria Evans, Lindenwold, NJ, USA
Former interior decorator, daughter of the King, age ninety-one

♥ In Memoriam ♥

Sweet Gloria walked by faith and was a testimony to all who knew her. On June 11, 2020, less than a month after writing this story, Gloria woke up and saw the face of Jesus whom she loved and served. She is greatly missed, but we have the hope of seeing her again one day in Heaven.

"My chains are gone,
I've been set free.
My God, my Savior has ransomed me,
And like a flood, His mercy rains;
Unending love, amazing grace."
- Chris Tomlin

STORY 74
GOD IS NOT DONE WITH ME YET!

As a young, recent college graduate, I was hired as a teacher at a local daycare. Three years later, I had been handpicked as the new director. From the beginning, I was determined to be confident and accomplish goals using the same qualities that had brought me this promotion. But soon I realized this job would require more of me than I had to give. Still, I persevered, and with every day I prayed for strength to push on.

I was dealing with situations every day that triggered a great level of anxiety—more than in all my years managing my anxiety disorder. I wore the word *anxiety* as if it were written on my forehead. Eventually I resigned, and *anxiety* was replaced with *failure*. I was a college graduate, unemployed, and far from where I thought I should be.

About this time, COVID-19 made its mark and everything shut down. I was left alone, believing I was a failure. My husband, always full of kindness and compassion, was not content to let me wear *failure*. He encouraged me to create a routine and stick to it every day. He knew I needed a perspective change, but I would not find it unless I had some motivation. Now my new routine begins every day with reading a chapter from the Bible.

One morning, the Lord brought me this verse: "He who began a good work in you will bring it to completion . . ." (Phil. 1:6 ESV). God showed me that I was so distracted by what I wanted to do and be, that I had completely lost sight of who God created me to be. I am not a failure because I am not the one who defines me. Only God defines who I am, and God is not done with me yet!

Now I know that real success comes from believing and acting in what God is doing in our lives. We can have confidence that the God who saved us has never stopped working on us. Therefore, we can look forward to a life filled with the Lord's success.

"And I am sure of this, that he who began a good work in you will bring it to completion at the day of Jesus Christ."—Philippians 1:6 ESV

Casey Arsenault, Xenia, OH, USA
Follower of Christ, and wife to Ryan

STORY 75
ROOT BEER FLOATS

As a teacher of thirty-three years, I can recall many instances of hanging on to hope, even when the world seemed to be shutting down. During my first year of teaching, in January 1986, the space shuttle Challenger exploded. In April 1995, the Oklahoma City bombing happened. And I will never forget September 11, 2001, when my students entered the classroom telling me that planes had crashed into the Twin Towers and America was at war.

In addition to these events, other catastrophes have happened including many school shootings. It seems the world is going crazy. None of these incidents, though, changed my career like COVID-19.

March 6, 2020 was a regular school day. Everyone was excited about the start of spring break and eagerly discussed plans. We enjoyed being together. My science students had just taken a test on the states of matter, followed by root beer floats as we said our goodbyes. Little did we know it was going to be the last time we would be together this school year.

We soon began to hear of social events being shut down. Colleges were sending students home and switching to online learning. Restaurants were offering only drive-through or take-out services. Public and private schools began to close. Now I was discovering a whole new world of virtual learning. These changes were stressful to educators, students, and their families.

I had been an educator for decades, and now had to adapt to new ways of teaching my students. My career began years before this current technology was introduced. I had some training and had been able to incorporate some technology into my lessons, but now everything would have to be done online. I had to learn and learn quickly. There was no time to waste.

One of the most valuable lessons God impressed on me during this time was that He is still in control. I had plans for how the 2019-2020 school year would end, but God's plans are higher. His ways are always good, and we can always trust Him to do what is best.

"For I know the plans I have for you," declares the Lord, "plans to prosper you and not to harm you, plans to give you hope and a future. Then you will call on me and come and pray to me, and I will listen to you. You will seek me and find me when you seek me with all your heart."—Jeremiah 29:11-13 NIV

Tammy Mantz, Houston, TX, USA
Wife, mother and Christian schoolteacher

STORY 76
GOD IS SOVEREIGN

On March 28, 2020, I received a text message that broke my heart and threatened to shatter my hopes for my upcoming marriage. We already knew our state was about to shut down because of COVID-19. We knew the uncertainty of quarantine would change our wedding plans. But this distressing text was about a good friend of mine. He had just passed away from a malignant brain tumor. The tumor had been discovered only two weeks prior. This was very sudden.

The tragedy, in addition to this terrible loss, was that he and his wife had only been married a few years, and they were in their forties. I had already watched my mother die of cancer in her forties, leaving my father behind. For someone on the brink of marriage, this was desperately sad news. It just served as another brick on top of my already sturdy wall of skepticism about living a long life with my soon-to-be husband.

Because of this virus, many people have passed into eternity—people with families, friends, spouses. Psalm 90:3-6 says that God makes mankind return to dust with a word. We are like a blade of grass that withers in the same day it sprouts. My friend's death reminded me powerfully that God is the master of our souls. We do not own the people we love. We cannot keep them with us any more than anything else God has given us. Everything belongs to Him as the Creator. It is God alone who forms light and creates darkness. He brings peace and salvation, but He also creates calamity.

This may seem discouraging, but the truth is that God's sovereignty is the greatest joy and comfort imaginable. This Deity we worship has complete power. He accomplishes all that He pleases, and yet He deals with us in lovingkindness and mercy. Give thanks today for the blessings that God has poured out upon you. Hold them with open hands toward

His plan and the promise of eternity, knowing that we do not own tomorrow.

"I form the light and create darkness, I bring prosperity and create disaster; I, the Lord, do all these things. You heavens above, rain down my righteousness; let the clouds shower it down. Let the earth open wide, let salvation spring up, let righteousness flourish with it; I, the Lord, have created it."—Isaiah 45:7-8 NIV

Lydia Pearson Kaufman, Charlotte, NC, USA
Student, writer, and newlywed

STORY 77
DIVINE APPOINTMENT

So peaceful—and then came John! It was the Thursday before Easter and I walked the short distance from home to the shopping centre for some groceries. "Oh, how peaceful and quiet it is," I mused. As I entered the mall, to my surprise, it looked as though I was the only person there. Almost every shop was closed. I could hardly believe the quietness and serenity of it all!

Walking to the grocery store, I bumped into John. We had spoken many times. He is on a disability pension and spends a lot of time there. Two days before, I had seen him and wished him a blessed Easter. Today he was sitting on a long bench near the elevators and so I sat down, observing the required social-distancing rules!

"Hi, John. It's lovely to see you again. Today is Easter Thursday. Do you know what Easter is really about?"

"Yes," he replied. "It's about God sending His Son to die on the cross for our sins and then rising again."

"That's right," I said, "I learned about that as a little girl, but I never really prayed to receive Jesus as my personal Saviour, not till I was much older. Have you ever thought about doing that?"

"No," he replied simply. "But I think I'd like to."

I told him I'd lead him in a short prayer, making sure he understood that it wasn't the prayer that would save him. He had to believe the words in his heart. John did indeed pray the prayer with me. As I was leaving, I told him that now he would have the most wonderful Easter he had ever had!

Sometimes, my dear friends, it's as simple as that. Now I am following up with John whenever I see him in the mall, and I make sure to give him materials that will help him grow in his faith.

Thanks to the shutdown and the quietness, a simple trip to buy a loaf of bread became a divine appointment!

"I charge you therefore before God and the Lord Jesus Christ, who will judge the living and the dead at His appearing and His kingdom: Preach the word! Be ready in season and out of season . . ."—2 Timothy 4:2 NKJV

Margaret Dorothy Woods, Sydney, Australia
Ministry representative's wife, supporter, and best friend!
Mother of four, and "Oma" of eight

STORY 78
ADDY WALKS

"Come on, Addy. It's time for a walk."

Because of the COVID-19 quarantine, I began a new work-from-home routine. While this created certain challenges, it also provided some opportunities, including having time to take walks. I try to take our little dog, Addy, for walks with me in the afternoon. She often gets distracted; smelling the grass, listening to other dogs bark, checking out each mailbox, heading back the way we came, and so on. My walks with Addy often take a lot longer than walks by myself.

On one of my walks I realized that I was a lot like Addy with God. God knows the quickest and most direct way to get to the goals He has for me. He wants me to become like Christ in my heart, my words, and my actions. Yet I, like Addy, get distracted by things that aren't really very important. I tug on the *leash* of God's instruction and head off in other directions. His Word, like the leash, is meant to keep me close, but I often chafe at the restrictions. If I didn't keep Addy on a leash, she would run into the street and wander off where she would get hurt or lost. God's leash, in the same way, keeps me from getting hurt by sin and Satan's devices. When Addy is trotting along beside me, the leash is hardly felt, and we move along quickly to our destination. In the same way, when I am walking with God, I don't feel limited. I enjoy being with Him and feeling His presence and guidance as He leads me safely along a path that takes me where He wants me to go.

"And this is love: that we walk in obedience to his commands. As you have heard from the beginning, his command is that you walk in love."—2 John 1:6 NIV

Dan Pearson, Erial, NJ, USA
IT Director and Addy's "Dad"

STORY 79
SAYING GOODBYE

"Don't worry. You'll see your friends again at graduation!" I kept reminding myself, trying to hold onto hope. Everything happened very quickly. I had to pack up all my things to leave campus on short notice, and it was heartbreaking. With all the thoughts racing through my mind, the weight of everything was indescribable.

The premature goodbyes were difficult. I tried to be optimistic, but my hope was diminishing with every day I spent at home. I began to process the fact that my senior year of college had ended without my friends. I did what I could to stay in touch, balance my course load, and cope with my cabin fever.

Then the long-awaited news came that my campus would be honoring the Class of 2020 virtually, with no traditional graduation ceremony. I think that's when reality set in. My college experience ended in a way that was not according to plan. I wasn't going to see my friends.

That's when I realized I had been so defiant in processing the truth, I hadn't left any room for God. He was there all along to show me His love through the entire process. When I was at my weakest moment, I remembered that God was and is all knowing and faithful. He knew about COVID-19 and the way it would affect college seniors since before our lives began. He knew we would have to say goodbye to our friends and be away from the relationships we created over the past four years.

My graduation ceremony was beautiful. I was happy to celebrate in the best way my college could provide. I'm not certain why things had to happen this way, but God has always been in control. I am hopeful He will make a way for the seniors to reunite and be able to say their official goodbyes. Until then, Father, allow me to realize that Your ways are not my own, and that You are bigger than all of us. You will keep us.

"Trust in the Lord with all your heart; do not depend on your own understanding. Seek his will in all you do, and he will show you which path to take."—Proverbs 3:5-6 NLT

Kierstyn Woody, Millsboro, DE, USA
Recent college graduate in music

STORY 80
PRACTICE

Have you noticed that the more you practice something, the better you become? This pandemic wasn't hard for me. You see, I had already had practice. My *practice run* came in 2001, when my husband, Martin, and I were taken hostage while doing missionary work in the Philippines. For more than a year, we lived in the jungle with terrorists, waiting for our release. The key word here is *waiting*—waiting for something good to happen. In our thirteenth month of captivity, my husband was killed in the gun battle that rescued me.

A pandemic and being held hostage can be very similar.

- They both came out of nowhere. We were caught off guard. No one plans on a pandemic—or being taken hostage.
- We suddenly lost our freedom and were told what to do. Stay indoors. Wash your hands. Disinfect everything. Wear a mask!—We were also told what to do in the jungle. Sit here. Eat this. Pee there. Be quiet!
- We were surrounded by a deadly enemy, a virus that we didn't understand.—We were surrounded by treacherous men with deadly M-16s.
- We were cut off from those we love and fearful, not knowing how long this trial would last.—Waiting, waiting, waiting to be set free and get back to normal. You get the point.

I learned to trust God in my hostage waiting experience. I really think that we learn things from what we suffer! I look back and see that God built a resilience in me that I didn't even know was possible. I've learned to love life as it is, not as I wish it to be. So, as I shelter in place in my little apartment in Kansas, I am able to see my COVID-19 isolation as a time to rest, to do things I never get to do, to slow down, sing, clean out closets and pray.

This is why I look at this pandemic as another practice. You see, my waiting isn't over. I'm waiting for the day when our Only Hope, Jesus, returns to get us, and all will be well.

"Therefore I will look unto the Lord; I will wait for the God of my salvation: my God will hear me."—Micah 7:7 KJV

Gracia Burnham, Rose Hill, KS, USA
Author, *In the Presence of My Enemies*
Missionary, Ethnos360

"For God so loved the world, that he gave his only begotten Son, that whosoever believeth in him should not perish, but have everlasting life."
—John 3:16 KJV

BIBLIOGRAPHY

Arlen, Harold, composer. "Follow the Yellow Brick Road." *The Wizard of Oz*, Edgar Yipsel Harburg, lyricist. Metro Goldwyn Mayer, 1939.

Card, Michael. "Wilderness Worth-Ship." Essay. *In A Sacred Sorrow: Reaching out to God in the Lost Language of Lament*, 21–24. United States, CO: The Navigators, 2014.

Chaiklin, Rebecca, and Eric Goode. Whole. *Tiger King*. Netflix, Inc., 2020.

E.T., the Extraterrestrial. Directed by Steven Spielberg. Los Angeles, CA: Universal City Studies, Inc., 1982.

Garrison, Greg. "What Clergy Said When Influenza Closed Churches in 1918." AL.com, April 17, 2020. www.al.com/coronavirus/2020/04/ what-clergy-said-when-influenza-closed-churches-in-1918.html.

Groundhog Day. Directed by Harold Ramis. USA: Columbia Pictures, 1993.

Guesstures, Pawtucket, RI. Hasbro Gaming, 2018. Board Game.

Haggard, Merle. "One Day at a Time." *Songs for the Mama That Tried*, MCA Records, 1981.

Mario Kart 8 Deluxe, Nintendo, 2017. https://mariokart8.nintendo.com/

Martin, Civilla D. "His Eye is on the Sparrow." (1905. Public Domain.)

Miles, C. Austin. "In the Garden." Hymnary.org. The Hymn Society, 2007. https://hymnary.org/text/i_come_to_the_garden_alone.

Moen, Don. "God Will Make A Way." We Are Worship, 2015. https://www.weareworship.com/us/songs/view/god-will-make-a-way-2430/4676/lyrics.

Original Soundtrack - The Sound of Music. RCA Victor, 1965.

Paxton, Gary S., "A Vessel of Honor for God." *Terminally Weird but Godly Right*, Pax Musical Reproductions, 1978.

Pearson, Bonnie R., "Like A Sunday in the Park." Poem, 2020.

Pearson, Bonnie R., and Mariano Jose Jimenez. "Hold Me in Your Hope." 2020.

"Quarantine." Merriam-Webster.com Dictionary, Merriam-Webster, https://www.merriam-webster.com/dictionary/quarantine. Accessed 8 Jun. 2020.

Quiplash, Jackbox Games, 2015. www.jackboxgames.com/party-pack-two/

"Set-apart." YourDictionary. LoveToKnow. www.yourdictionary.com/set-apart.

Sielaff, Vivian. "Tea Anyone? ~ Garden Tea Party ~." Holy Moments with God, June 22, 2020. https://viviansielaff.wordpress.com/2014/03/19/tea-anyone-garden-tea-party/.

The Game of Scattergories, Pawtucket, RI. Hasbro, 2018. Board Game.

The Sound of Music: Original Broadway Cast. Sony BMG Music Entertainment, 1959.

Tomlin, Chris, Louie Giglio, "Amazing Grace (My Chains Are Gone)." *See The Morning*, Six Step Records, 2006.

"Who We Are." Chick-fil-A, 2020. https://www.chick-fil-a.com/about/who-we-are.

CPSIA information can be obtained
at www.ICGtesting.com
Printed in the USA
BVHW031312101220
595373BV00018B/86

9 781664 208391